. S
w

D1320560

The Scanlon Plan For Organization Development: Identity, Participation, and Equity

$\mathcal{MS70}$

THE SCANLON PLAN
FOR ORGANIZATION
DEVELOPMENT:
IDENTITY, PARTICIPATION,
AND EQUITY

CARL F. FROST

JOHN H. WAKELEY

ROBERT A. RUH

MICHIGAN STATE UNIVERSITY PRESS

1974

44 06 91

Copyright © 1974

MICHIGAN STATE UNIVERSITY PRESS

Library of Congress Card Catalog Number: 74–75366

ISBN: *0–87013–184–2*

MANUFACTURED IN THE UNITED STATES OF AMERICA

★
  ★
★
  ★

  ★

TO

Evelyn

John AND *Winnie*

George, Virginia AND *Pam*

HD
2971
.F76
1974

Contents

Foreword

In 1942 Douglas McGregor presented a seminar for the clinical psychology interns at Worcester State Hospital, where he had earlier received his clinical training. The applications of the clinical psychological principles to industrial organizations were obvious and challenging.

Upon the completion of military service in 1946, it was good fortune and coincidence that Douglas McGregor's personal encouragement brought me to Massachusetts Institute of Technology as a research associate. Douglas McGregor was working on his Theory X and Theory Y observations toward his book, *The Human Side of Enterprise.*

Concurrently, Kurt Lewin, the stimulating theorist who was developing the basic principles and vectors of group dynamics, Joseph N. Scanlon, the innovating practitioner who was leading management and labor into unique cooperative relationships to achieve surprising levels of productivity, and Clinton S. Golden, the pioneering labor advocate who was stressing the causes of industrial peace rather than conflict, arrived at M.I.T. These men began informally to exchange with staff and students their convictions and commitments regarding the importance and potential influence of people.

Having my early degree in cost accounting proved to be a convenient skill for Joe Scanlon in carrying out the historical analyses of organizations seeking industrial peace, productivity, and sound profitability. The genius and parsimony of the principles of Joe Scanlon's cooperative productivity concept in organizational development were clear from the beginning. The psychological soundness of the principles became increasingly apparent in the various early applications of the Scanlon Plan at LaPointe Machine Tool Company, Market Forge, Tubular Rivet, Towle Silver Company, Cox Foundry, Stromberg-Carlson, to name only a few organizations.

That the innovative concept should have the designation of the Scanlon Plan is most appropriate, and yet inconsistent with the modesty of its author. It was a functional accident that originated the name. When the first conference was being convened for those organizations that had written for information regarding the productivity incentive system, it was necessary to post directional arrows from the Massachusetts Avenue entrance of

M.I.T. through the mechanical engineering laboratories to the Economics and Industrial Relations Section of Charles Myers. What should be the title designation on the arrows? After some resistance Joe agreed to have the "Scanlon Conference" crayoned on the arrows. He did not believe the idea would have wide circulation or lasting usage.

The current distribution throughout the United States, England, somewhat intensively in the Netherlands, and in Europe contradicts his early aspirations for the concept. The applications in a wide range of industrial organizations as well as hospitals and schools far exceed his modest expectations.

When Michigan State University extended me the invitation to join their faculty in 1949, the consultation role to industry was novel in this first land grant institution which had established an illustrative reputation in the traditional agricultural programs extended to farmers. President John A. Hannah, a dynamic institution builder and national and international land grant innovator, was intrigued with the possibilities of the linkage of the University to Michigan industries through the organizational development of the Scanlon Plan. He wanted one primary assurance: that the industrial organizations would receive the high quality of professional service that the farmers had always received from Michigan State University staff and that the academic disciplines would be advanced by the study and research available in these Scanlon Plan operating organizations. President Hannah commissioned loyal alumni to check and assure him of the validity and reliability of the Scanlon Plan programs.

Twenty years of consultation, study, and research have verified the soundness of the original Scanlon Plan principles. The multiple applications have demonstrated the Scanlon Plan's versatility. The organizational development, productivity, and profitability have shown the potentials of the program.

The primary psychological emphases of the studies have isolated three conditions which are essential to the effective organization: identification of the company and the employees' roles within it; the opportunity for all employees to participate and to become responsible; and the economic and psychological equity of all employees. These conditions include the psychological, social, and economic factors which can meet the needs of the individual employee in his personal and professional self-actualization within the work-life situation. These conditions also meet the employees' corporate needs to belong and to participate responsibly in developing a viable, competitive, and fiscally sound organization. These conditions develop the individual's and the organization's ability and potential to anticipate and implement the insistent demand for improvement and change.

This book is the consequence of twenty-five years of experimenting and exploring the principles and applications of the Scanlon Plan.

The first two chapters are presented by Dr. John Wakeley, a 1961 graduate of Michigan State University, who chose to see the world of industrial and organizational life at Corning Glass Works before returning to MSU in 1964. From his experience and continual consultation with industrial, health, and governmental organizations, the focus for the need, relevance, and readiness for the Scanlon Plan is directed to the organizational managers and leaders.

In the next three chapters, I present the three psychological conditions as they have been observed and programmed in many organizations over the twenty-five year period. This material includes not only the principles but also the specific procedures, their function, and relevance to the successful implementation by the operating managers and the mature executive leadership.

The sixth and seventh chapters are written by Dr. Robert Ruh, a Michigan State University graduate of 1970. He executed a major Scanlon Plan research study in his doctoral program and then continued an intensive pursuit of the primary conditions basic to the Scanlon Plan. In the sixth chapter he reviews the research that is related to the most promising theories and principles of organizational development. This material gives the operating manager an evaluation of the research findings to date and how he might interpret and apply the findings in his own participative style of management. In the final chapter, Dr. Ruh points out the research which would be advantageous and significant to pursue in advancing the art and science of participative management as promoted by the Scanlon Plan.

This book is not a textbook in the strictly academic usage of the term. It is written to and for the many personal, professional, and managerial colleagues in all organizations who are interested in effective management, whether they are currently exploiting or investigating the principles and potentials of the Scanlon Plan. Without their continued assistance and challenge and without the availability of their organizational laboratories, these pages could not have been written. We are indeed grateful to all of them.

We acknowledge the special encouragement and assistance of the Scanlon

Plan Associates, their board of directors, and their member companies. We also acknowledge the stimulation of colleagues and students. We thank Ms. Nancy Hammond for her help with the form and substance of the work.

The fortuitous encounter and tutelage of such self-effacing giants as Douglas McGregor and Joe Scanlon remains an unpaid debt of gratitude.

CARL F. FROST

CHAPTER 1

Background and Getting Started

THE SCANLON PLAN is a philosophy, a theory of organization, and a set of management principles. As a philosophy, the Scanlon Plan rests on the assumptions that people prefer to express themselves fully in all situations including work situations and that, when they do express themselves, they can be constructive and supportive of other people and the groups to which they belong. The theory which follows from this position states that the basic philosophy is best served when all members of an organization participate as fully as they can in the activities of the organization and when they are equitably rewarded for their participation. All principles of management that encourage people to identify with their work group, that encourage people to participate as much as they can, and that continually focus on equitably rewarding all members of the organization are seen as ways of applying the Scanlon Plan philosophy.

This mixture of philosophy, theory, and application makes it difficult—indeed inappropriate—to define the Scanlon Plan in any but the broadest terms. In its specific applications, the Scanlon Plan is usually quite different from one company to another. Companies may start with full commitment to the total philosophy and theory. Some may have little commitment to the abstract bases of the plan but be convinced that the management principles involved are sound and worth application. Still others may simply be fiddling around, following the Joneses, or experimenting. As in most practical applications of theory and philosophy, the success of the application depends on the validity of the assumptions *and* on the commitment within the organization to the assumptions and the desire to make them work. When the plan is successful, the organization is effective in all its operations and each member of the organization is effective in his working life. Any organization that tries to implement a Scanlon Plan does so not with the goal of making a particular set of ideas succeed but with the central goal of improving the performance of the organization.

Historical Survey

The history of the Scanlon Plan spans most of the years of the human relations movement in industry. Its initial applications and successes were hailed as models for labor-management relations and human relations within organizations. Its most recent applications are models for applying modern management principles and for organization development.

In the 1930s Joe Scanlon worked for a steel mill which, like many other companies in those difficult depression years, was facing the prospect of going out of business. Equipment was obsolete, the market for its product was small and its own share of the market uncertain, profits were almost nil, and employees were seeking improved working conditions and higher wages. As a union leader in the plant, Scanlon convinced top management, his fellow workers, and the international union to try cooperative efforts to meet the problems. The union agreed not to press its demands for higher wages immediately, and management agreed to increase wages when improved productivity made increases possible. After Scanlon and others on a special committee had talked with workers throughout the plant, the employees agreed to make an all-out effort to improve productivity. Once the workers' cooperation had been enlisted, their knowledge of the processes and suggestions for improving the operation were successful in reducing costs, decreasing waste, improving efficiency, and improving quality. After a few months the cooperation between workers and management paid off. The survival of the company was assured, and the employees received increased wages and improved working conditions.

After the success of his approach became apparent, Scanlon took a staff position with the United Steelworkers Union and began promulgating the principles as a sound basis for union-management relations. The central idea was to foster cooperation rather than competition between union and management without undermining the collective bargaining process or agreement. Many participants in union-management relations and most observers of the scene had argued that cooperation was a better model than competition. Their arguments were generally abstract and hypothetical. On the other hand, Scanlon tried to make cooperation tangible and specific. Emphasis was placed on what was happening in the organization now and how cooperation between labor and management might improve conditions. How can cooperation improve operations, reduce costs, and improve work flow? How can cooperation improve the company's chances of survival and lead to more take-home pay for all employees? The specifics of accounting systems might vary, but all members of an organization were paid as a function of the overall productivity of the company. The specifics for going all-out to improve productivity might vary, but each member of the organization had a voice in how he did his job, and all members were represented at meetings with the highest company management. Employee representatives and management cooperated to improve productivity and to share the benefits.

After a few years at the central offices of the United Steelworkers, Scanlon was invited to join the staff at Massachusetts Institute of Technology as a lecturer. He accepted but, while instructing others in the specifics and advantages of cooperation, he continued his activities in the field.

Joe Scanlon's personality and charisma helped to insure the success of applications of the plan. He was an ex-boxer, a cost accountant, a steel worker, a union leader, and an MIT lecturer. He could talk to and understand both workers and management, and they could understand him. He had the common touch of a common man, the ideas of a fine intellect, and the appeal and conviction of a good man with a sound message. The essence of the plan continued even after his death in 1956. Likewise, applications of the plan continued. Some had thought that Joe Scanlon was the person essential to the plan's success; the thought was groundless.

In 1950 *Fortune* magazine published an article "Enterprise for Everyman," by R. Davenport, which recounted the success of the Scanlon Plan at the LaPointe Machine Tool Company. The article emphasized the positive effects of cooperation and stressed that the basis of cooperation was participation by all members of the organization in achieving the company's goals. In the years since the publication of "Enterprise for Everyman," the

3

Scanlon Plan has had the continuing attention of people who had been associated with Joe Scanlon. Several people have stayed active in introducing companies to the plan and maintaining applications of the philosophy and theory.

Frederick Lesieur, who had been president of the union at the LaPointe Company, became the leading figure in applying the plan in the geographic area where Scanlon had operated. An annual conference of companies with the Scanlon Plan, or with interest in it, is held at MIT. One of these conferences, in 1958, was the basis for the only previous book, written by Lesieur, devoted entirely to the subject of the Scanlon Plan.

Another center of Scanlon activity has been developed at Michigan State University under the leadership of Dr. Carl Frost. Frost worked at MIT with Scanlon and left there to join the Psychology Department at Michigan State University in 1949. Since then he has been active in initiating and maintaining the Scanlon Plan in companies, primarily in Michigan, and in training industrial-organizational psychologists. Several of his students have remained interested in the plan in their research, teaching, or practice, and a few have worked at installing and maintaining plans in organizations.

In 1964, representatives from several companies with whom Dr. Frost had worked held a conference to explore common concerns. These companies and others with similar interests continued to hold annual meetings and, in 1968, eight companies from this group formed a non-profit corporation, the Midwest Scanlon Associates, later changed to Scanlon Plan Associates (SPA). Today SPA has a year-round program with varied objectives and activities. There are still annual conferences for companies with the plan and for companies interested in exploring application of the plan in their own operations. In addition, inter-company groups, such as first-line supervisors or financial executives, meet regularly for training programs and discussions of common concerns. Individual companies and the SPA as a group sponsor and participate in research activities for the purposes of developing improved understanding and application. For example, more than 2,600 people from all levels of six different companies responded to a survey questionnaire concerning attitudes toward the Scanlon philosophy and its application (see Chapter 7). Efforts to publicize the plan and interest other organizations in applying it are also part of the SPA's program.

During these years of gradually increasing application, the plan has received infrequent attention in the scholarly and professional literature.

References are scattered over the industrial relations, business and management, and psychological journals and periodicals. As mentioned earlier, only Lesieur's book in 1958 has been devoted exclusively to the topic. The literature that does exist is, for the most part, positive, concerning the intentions of the plan and its apparent ability to improve human relations and productivity within organizations. However, it is based primarily on case studies and personal experience and includes few systematic research reports (see Chapters 6 and 7).

Today, almost thirty-five years after Joe Scanlon's first efforts to promote cooperation as a means for improving a company's productivity and thus for insuring higher wages for the work force, the central mechanisms of cooperation and the basic philosophy remain useful. How is the plan implemented? What are the mechanisms for building cooperation, participation, and productivity improvement into organizations?

Mechanisms of the Plan

The plan has two sets of mechanisms for achieving its goals. One set attempts to insure that all members of an organization have the opportunity to participate in improving productivity; the other attempts to insure that equitable rewards for improving productivity will come to all members of the organization. Clearly, the mechanisms are not the whole plan. If an organization adopts the mechanisms without significant commitment by management and the workers to the philosophy of cooperation and participation, the goals of the plan are not likely to be achieved and the mechanisms themselves are likely to fail.

As they must, to reflect the history and special operations of the companies, the specifics of these mechanisms vary widely from one company to another. In fact, one company has changed these mechanisms so much that their particular application would not agree with the description below in any particular. However, even this company started with a plan that was close to the general description. More importantly, the changes that this company has made have always been for the purpose of improving cooperation and have been arrived at by cooperative, participative methods. Thus, changing the mechanisms has better defined the philosophy of human relations, the theory of organization, and the principles of management essential to the plan.

The descriptions of the mechanisms presented below illustrate how the

5

plan has been and can be implemented; they do not prescribe how it must be done. These descriptions are greatly simplified. Additional descriptions and added detail can be found in later chapters, especially in Chapters 3, 4, and 5.

THE PARTICIPATION SYSTEM

What are the mechanisms to facilitate the improvement of productivity? What paths can an organization take to the goal and its associated rewards?

The participation system is based on the assumption that, if productivity is to increase, something must change. While much has been said about resistance to change and the many problems of bringing about change, the Scanlon Plan treats change as a common and natural state of affairs. Change is treated as inevitable, and attention is directed toward controlling the rate and direction of change and toward communicating the advantages and results of change throughout the organization. Wide participation in suggesting, in deciding about, and in carrying out change is encouraged.

There are two main features to the participation system for changing conditions and improving productivity—an open suggestion system and a committee structure for encouraging, evaluating, acting on, and communicating the actions taken on suggestions. These two features are closely related and will be presented simultaneously.

As a part of implementing a Scanlon Plan, two kinds of committees are established within the organization. At one level are the Production Committees. In each department (or other appropriate subunit of the company) a Production Committee of one management representative and one or more elected representatives is established. The management representative is usually the supervisor of the department, and the other representatives are elected by the people (nonmanagerial) who work within the department. The election procedure is intended to identify the best spokesman within each department and also over a period of time to afford many people in the department the opportunity to learn about the committee's responsibilities and work through firsthand experience. To accomplish these two goals of high quality and broad participation, the organization may adopt procedures, such as staggered terms for elected representatives to make sure that an experienced representative is on the committee at all times, or no more than two consecutive terms for any representative.

Each Production Committee has two major responsibilities. The members are to encourage people to make productivity-improving suggestions and to take action on the suggestions once they are made. Typically, appropriate forms are provided for writing suggestions in multiple copies, so that the originator(s) of the idea may keep a copy and one or more copies may go forward for evaluation. At a very basic level, the committees explain the use of the forms and help people complete them. More importantly, the committees encourage people to make suggestions by identifying problems which interfere with increasing productivity and by urging all members of the unit to examine their own jobs with an eye on how to do them better. The relationship of improved productivity to bonuses is stressed. People do not receive individual financial reward for suggestions, but the fact of helping everyone in the company, including oneself, by doing one's own job better is emphasized. All ideas that may improve productivity are encouraged. For example, ideas about material handling and flow, improved equipment, different groupings of people to perform tasks, improved maintenance, special jigs, and so forth are all solicited. The central idea is that the person doing the job will have good ideas for doing the work better, can share those ideas with people who do the same or similar work, and will encourage other people to make suggestions by sharing ideas with them.

Each Production Committee meets periodically, every two to four weeks, to determine any specific problem areas where suggestions would be particularly helpful and to consider all suggestions made since the last meeting. In reviewing suggestions, the committee has four options: (1) it can put the suggestion into effect immediately; (2) it can seek more information or clarification about the suggestion; (3) it can pass the suggestion to the Screening Committee; or (4) it can reject the suggestion. Usually ideas for improvement which require interdepartmental action or which require large amounts of money to implement are referred to the Screening Committee. What is a large amount of money depends on the particular company; $100 per idea might be a ceiling in one company, and $500 might be the ceiling in another. All ideas involving purchases of major equipment are referred to the Screening Committee.

The Screening Committee is composed of the heads of major functional areas—for example, the chief executive officer, the chief financial officer, the chief production officer, the chief sales executive, and the chief engineer (titles of these people will vary from company to company), and an equal or greater number of elected, nonmanagerial, nonsupervisory people. Meetings of the committee are held once each month just before the time when bonuses are to be paid. In meeting its responsibilities, the committee oper-

7

ates by consensus and seeks to avoid binding votes on the one hand and unilateral action by management on the other. As a consequence of this way of operating, an exact balance of managerial and elected representatives is not necessary, and in many plans the elected representatives outnumber the managers.

As mentioned, one responsibility of the Screening Committee is to take action on all suggestions which are not put into effect by the Production Committee. Other responsibilities include reviewing the financial data used to determine whether a bonus is to be paid for the month just completed and announcing the bonus (or no bonus) and supporting information to all members of the company. Finally, the committee identifies problems and encourages all employees to make suggestions as to how to meet those problems. Detailed minutes of the meetings are seldom kept, but the disposition of suggestions, facts about the bonus, and significant information about the company's operations and problems are recorded and distributed to the entire company.

Most suggestions made within a month are acted on within that same month. Frequently, they are put into effect immediately by the Production Committees or, after review, by the Screening Committee. Those which are rejected are returned to the initiator along with the reasons for the rejection. The explanation of why an idea was rejected is done on a person-to-person basis by a member of either the appropriate Production Committee or of the Screening Committee. Some suggestions may require a staff study or may be held for implementation at a later (specific) time. All suggestions are accounted for periodically, perhaps every six to twelve months, to insure that all are acted on and to provide information to all people in the company about the operations of the suggestion system.

The committee structure encourages suggestions and provides a participative decision-making system to evaluate the proposed changes on their merits for improving productivity and on their feasibility, given the present realities of time, money, people, and problem restraints facing the company. It also helps to focus the fact that removing practical restraints may be the key to improving productivity and thus generating better bonus. The sweeper, the president, and all in between have ready access to a system that will judge ideas and report back exactly what can be done with the ideas now. All people have equal opportunity to learn about the variety of practical problems that slow down improvements. People find tangible, immediate examples of the intangible abstractions that frequently pass for communication within organizations. A company statement that "our poor profit position precludes production expansion" is made specific when people know that there is $10,000 available now and it seems more sensible to spend it on the maintenance of present equipment to guarantee present productivity levels rather than buy a new machine which would help them produce more if they could depend on the equipment they already have. The staff man's report "that perverse machine operators in the Polishing Department are failing to meet the engineering standards set for their equipment" is investigated and facts uncovered that the fault is with the process for delivering stock to the machines. The process is operating in spurts rather than in the continuous way that is necessary if the machines are to have the long runs on which the engineering standard is based.

As committee members become adept at processing suggestions, learn the standards of merit and feasibility for evaluating change, and learn to accept and trust each other, they are also operating as a communication system. The structure of the system puts first-line supervisors and employees, as well as highest management and employees, in face-to-face contact. Periodic elections insure that all employees have a chance to become part of the structure. The content of the communication concerns production, productivity improvement, change, financial information, and bonuses. This content is significant to all members of the organization and requires that the face-to-face contact be concerned with working, not with sociability. Finally, the system is evaluated frequently. Are suggestions acted on quickly? Are reports of bonuses and the supporting information clear? Are explanations about rejected suggestions understandable?

As the participation system succeeds in encouraging all members to invest more of themselves and their ideas in the organization, the company's effectiveness is increased. A second set of mechanisms, the Equity System, provides that all members of the organization can keep track of their investments and share in any bonuses generated by the productivity improvements. The discussion presented below is a simplified one; for a more complete discussion, see Chapter 5.

THE EQUITY SYSTEM

Basic to the Equity System is the assumption, or axiom, that people in organizations should be fairly rewarded for their contributions to the organization. To the extent that a person invests his time, talent, and career in an organization, he should receive a fair return on that investment. To the

9

extent that people invest themselves in working *together* to accomplish the goals and purposes of the organization, they should receive a fair return on their investment.

Each person is different in the particular combination of skills and talents he or she brings to an organization. The basic wage and salary structure should be fair; people in jobs requiring more skill and in jobs more important to the total organization should receive more pay than people in lesser jobs. Concurrently, within similar jobs, long-service people should receive more pay than short-service people because they have more invested. The individual as an individual with special background, skills, and contributions to make must be fairly paid for his unique services to the organization. Wage and salary structures recognize the fact of individual differences and attempt to reward these differences.

While people are different, they do need to work together if they are to accomplish the goals of the organization. What are the incentive systems for rewarding cooperation? Clearly all the individual piece-rate systems emphasize individuality and competition. If a person develops a technique for working faster or more efficiently, he can make more money than he made formerly. Further, if he keeps the new technique to himself, he can make more money than others doing the same job. There is financial incentive to improve productivity, but there is no financial incentive to disseminate the improvement. Cooperation is not rewarded by the organization and may be costly to the pieceworker.

An example from the shoe industry illustrates the "everyone-for-himself-and-don't-worry-about-the-last-in-line" spirit of individual incentive plans. The lasting department was continuously processing a variety of styles and sizes of shoes. All members of the department worked on an individual piece rate. By custom, the senior person in the group was at the head of the line and took first choice as shoes entered the department; he picked off as many of the easier, higher paying jobs as he could. Members of the department were in order of seniority, and each took his pick of what was left. The youngest persons in the department "got the leavings," were usually not able to make much money, and generally left after a short time. Thus, with the steady flow of inexperienced people coming into the department, there were serious problems of quality and even some problems with the quantity of production. Clearly, there was no incentive for cooperation, and none occurred.

An illustration of how strong the spirit of the individual incentive can be comes from this same department. In an effort to encourage cooperation in solving the quality and quantity problems, management developed a job rotation plan, whereby members of the department took turns being first in line, second in line, and so forth. When the foreman of the department called the workers together and explained the new plan, the senior man in the department punched him in the mouth.

Incentives paid to small groups on the basis of *group* performance can overcome some problems of the individual incentive systems. Such systems do encourage cooperation within the group, but may lead to harmful competition and the refusal to share important information between groups.

In a furniture factory, the milling and machine departments were on regular wages, while the cabinet and finishing departments were on a group incentive system. Over a period of time the cabinet and finishing areas developed a high degree of cooperation and internal support based on the easily seen advantages of working together. The milling and machine areas also worked together well, based primarily on their dislike of the cabinet and finishing departments and on the belief that bonuses were being made "at their expense." There were virtually no informal, positive contacts between members of the two differently paid groups—no coffee breaks together, no lunches together, no bowling after work. Members from the finishing department would sometimes drop their bonus check stubs near the time clock and other places where they were sure "the machine boys will find them and suffer." Machine room workers would let material of marginal quality go through with the comment, "Let them work on this for a while and see if they can *earn* their money."

To promote cooperation throughout the organization, the Scanlon Plan provides a financial incentive to everyone in the organization based on the performance of the *total* organization. Thus, all members of the organization are encouraged to cooperate and share information about improvements. Competition to increase rewards is thus shifted from between individuals or between groups within the company to between the company and other companies in the same market. Shifting the emphasis does not immediately eliminate intra-organizational competition; it does create a new perspective for dealing with problems created by competition.

The mechanisms of the equity system try to guarantee that people will know how the company is doing and, that when improved productivity leads to bonuses, the bonuses will be fairly determined and equitably distributed.

11

The simplest form of Scanlon Plan ratio (bonus computation formula) compares the total cost of compensating people within the organization to the total market value of what the organization produces.

$$\frac{\text{total personnel costs (costs of compensating people)}}{\text{total value of production}}$$

Some organizations may use an expanded formula (see Chapter 5), which includes other costs in the numerator in addition to the personnel costs, such as materials and supplies, but however complicated the formula may be or grow to be over time, the basic ideas of the ratio remain the same. These basic ideas are that the ratio should be an accurate representation of the organization's operations, that it should be comprehensible and trustworthy to all members of the organization, and that it should serve as a common target—improving productivity is the common goal.

To establish the ratio, the organization undertakes a thorough review of its recent history. A month-by-month analysis of the most recent three to five years of a company's history of sales, production costs, personnel costs, and related figures is a typical way of proceeding. More important than the precise time period is the extent to which the period seems plausibly representative of the normal operation of the company. The period selected is preferably one in which the company was making a profit or at least breaking even. It is preferably a period during which personnel cost and product value were not subject to great fluctuations or abrupt change. For example, sudden changes in the costs of raw materials, major technological innovations, or severe fluctuations in the price structure for finished goods would all indicate that the time period may not be representative. To the extent that the history of the organization is free from dramatic events, the accounting techniques to establish the ratio are easier and generally free from controversial judgments. If the organization has not been profitable or if there have been dramatic events, then the judgment of company personnel and other experts (consultants) may be required to help insure that the ratio is a fair representation of healthy company operations. It is even possible to establish a ratio for a company that is just beginning and has no history. This would, of course, require considerable judgment and comparative information from similar kinds of companies. Once the ratio is set, the hope is that it will remain fixed for a long time. However, it is possible to adjust the ratio when circumstances dictate. The adjustments are arrived at by cooperative efforts of management and the other employees, using the Participation System discussed in an earlier section of this chapter. The basic purpose is not to preserve a particular ratio, but to preserve bilateral equity in a changing world.

Once the ratio is determined, it becomes the basis for a monthly computation to see whether a bonus can be paid. Figuring a ratio of personnel costs to the value of production that can be computed every month can cause problems, especially for job shop type operations or businesses that have great seasonal variability. However, the advantages of paying or not paying bonuses after a short time period generally outweigh the initial problems of setting the ratio. The advantages result from providing people with information about their work performance as close as possible to the time when they do the work, thus making a better bridge between doing the work and being rewarded for the work—prompt reinforcement of constructive learning. One of the effects of the Scanlon Plan is to create a situation in which people can learn more about the company and be in a better position to recommend improvements. Generally, people learn more and learn faster when they can get feedback-information about how they are doing.

Bonuses are paid when performance beats the ratio, that is, when personnel costs are a smaller percentage of the total value of production than in the base period. An initial ratio that is inaccurate or one that is technically accurate but not well understood by employees is apt to undermine the whole plan. Cooperation between management and employees and wide participation in determining the fairness of the ratio are vital to future success, and are an excellent learning experience for all concerned about how to work together on significant organizational problems. Assuming that it is accurate, a less sophisticated ratio that is understandable to all employees and perceived as fair is preferred to a more sophisticated but "suspicious" ratio.

Total people costs is the numerator of the ratio. What are the "people costs"? How much is "total"? *Total* means all the wages, salary, and benefits paid to every member of the company. When supervisors, managers, clerical personnel, production personnel, everyone in the company cooperate to improve productivity, everyone benefits. Communicating the idea that everyone benefits from cooperation is much more likely to succeed when one can say the ratio includes people "from the president to the floor sweeper" than when one must say that cooperation is good for everyone "except" the managers or the secretaries or some other special group.

Sales value of production is the denominator of the ratio. Procedures for determining this figure may vary widely from company to company. Companies producing large volumes of low item-cost products for immediate sale may be able to use sales figures adjusted for changes in finished inventory and have very accurate month-to-month information about the value of production. A job shop operation with a small volume of high item-cost products may need to develop several in-process measures in order to accurately assess the value of production for a short time period, such as a month. Whatever the basis for determining the value, the principles of fairness and understandability must be met by the final result.

THE BONUS

Once an accurate, fair, understandable, and acceptable ratio is available, the personnel costs and value of production for each month's operations are compared to the standard to determine whether a bonus should be paid. A simplified example shows how the bonus pool is obtained and the kinds of questions that need to be answered to insure equitable distribution of the bonus pool. (For a more detailed and "real" example see Chapter 5.)

If, in a certain company, the ratio is .40/1.00, that is $.40 people cost for each $1.00 of production value, and there is a production value of $100,000 for the month of June, then $40,000 is the expected people cost. However, if actual personnel costs are say $30,000, then $10,000 has been saved and becomes the bonus pool.

Equitable distribution of the bonus pool requires that three conditions be met: (1) the company as a company and the employees as a total group must receive fair shares of the bonus pool; (2) part of the bonus pool must be held in reserve to make up to the company any deficit (negative bonus) that might occur in a future month; (3) each individual member of the organization must receive a fair share of the pool.

These conditions might be met as shown in Table 1.

What constitutes an equitable share for a company must meet the standards of being fairly and openly determined and understood by the participants in the plan. While the company's share may be as much as forty to fifty percent, a large number of companies feel that no percent is the most equitable share. These companies that take nothing reason that since they profit from more efficient operations, greater receptivity to change, and generally good human relations, taking a share from the bonus pool would amount to two shares for the company and one for employees. The company share does, however, "take the heat off" the admittedly imperfect

TABLE 1
June Bonus Report

a. Scanlon ratio	.40/1.00
b. Value of production	$100,000
c. Expected costs (a × b)	40,000
d. Actual costs	30,000
e. Bonus pool (c − d)	10,000
f. Share to company—20% (e × .20)	2,000
g. Share to employees—80% (Adjusted pool) (e × .80)	8,000
h. Share for future deficits—25% of Adjusted pool (g × .25)	2,000
i. Pool for immediate distribution (g − h)	6,000
j. Bonus for each employee* as a percentage of his pay for the production period (i ÷ d)	20%

The June pay record might look like this for a typical employee.

Name	Monthly pay for June	Bonus %	Bonus	Total Pay
Mary Smith	$600	20%	$120	$720

*This example assumes that all employees are participating in the plan at the time this bonus is paid, e.g., there has been no turnover and no employees are in their initial 30-, 60-, or 90-day trial periods.

ratio, so that companies are less likely to change the ratio with every change from base period conditions.

What percentage of the bonus pool goes into the reserve, or contingency, fund to protect the company depends primarily on the stability of production, sales, and product mix over a year's operation. A relatively stable company that experiences little if any seasonal variation may take fifteen percent of the month's pool to meet "bad-month" contingencies. On the other hand, a highly seasonal organization which faces uncertain markets —for example, a producer of Christmas novelties, decorations, and toys— may put aside forty percent of the pool to meet contingencies. A usual percentage might be twenty to twenty-five percent. Once each year, usually on the anniversary date of initiating the plan, the contingency fund is reviewed. If there is a surplus, it is treated as an additional bonus pool, and the total pool is payed out as a year-end bonus. If there is a deficit, the company absorbs the deficit, and the new year begins with a clean slate. Obviously, if the contingency fund is large or there is a large deficit, the organization should review the Equity System and make any necessary adjustments.

The part of the bonus pool available for immediate distribution in any month will be a percentage of the actual personnel costs for that month, and that percentage is the bonus figure for each member of the organization. For each employee, the compensation received during the month on which the bonus pool is based is multiplied by the percentage. Equity is thus defined as each person's getting the same percentage bonus. This definition of equity depends on the existence of a sound, fair salary structure. While every employee gets the same percentage, the actual dollars each person receives depends on his base pay and how many hours he works. Five percent of the president's monthly salary will be more dollars than five percent of the monthly wages of the stock boy, and this is fair because, it is assumed, the president is making a bigger contribution to the company. However, if people are paid more or less than they are worth to the organization, the bonus will compound the problem of inequity, not solve it.

Providing a common goal is the beginning of cooperation. Everyone in the organization knows that by improving his productivity he helps to beat the ratio and to generate a tangible financial reward for the total effort. Thus, instead of working together only because cooperation is a "good idea," which is an intangible reason, people work together because it is a "good idea" *and* because there is an economic advantage to cooperation.

The Equity and the Participation mechanisms are ways of trying to implement and give tangibility to the Scanlon philosophy. It was stated earlier that the plan is not just the mechanisms; however, it is also true that without trustworthy mechanisms there could be no plan. Details of the mechanism—for example, the exact ratio, the percent to the contingency reserve, the number of committees, the ways of holding elections—are fitted to each particular company. Thus, no two companies need have the same Scanlon Plan. What the companies share is some commitment to the philosophy, theory, and broad management principles and some ways of implementing and testing the commitment every day against each day's reality.

Getting Started

Why do companies decide to adopt the Scanlon Plan and how do they get started? Specific answers to both these questions depend on the particular company; however, general answers exist for these questions, as do general guidelines for answering them specifically.

Companies try the Scanlon Plan either because they have identified problems in their operations and think that a suggestion system or a bonus system might help solve the problems or because they learn about the plan and want to "experiment." The problems that cause companies to seek a plan are frequently those of poor productivity and poor industrial relations. Organizations that see the plan as a solution may view the mechanisms as the heart of the plan. Managers in these companies may believe that paying people for ideas to improve productivity and meeting with people occasionally will solve problems no matter what philosophy of human relations they have. These managers will usually find that tension develops in a company when people are led to believe that they have opportunities to participate and cooperate and then discover that they have no real opportunities but only a "sense of" participation. Further, most managers will find that the tension makes it more difficult to solve problems and may even bring new problems. It is possible that the mechanisms may help teach participation and cooperation. In any case, it is true now, as it was in the original application by Joe Scanlon, that the problems are solved because people work in the spirit of the philosophy. This does not mean that it is necessary or perhaps even desirable to have an explicit statement of the organization's philosophy, theory of organization or management principles. What is required is that the behavior of all people in the company, managerial and nonmanagerial, be in accord with the basic philosophy of the plan.

Other companies adopt the plan not so much to solve particular problems as to have a vehicle for implementing ideas about how organizations should be run. These companies may hear about the plan and after investigation try it, or they may develop some general goals for their companies and find the bases and mechanisms of the Scanlon Plan are congruent with their ideas. Compatibility of abstract ideas does not insure success. The ways people behave with the problems of participation and equity, not the ways they talk about the problems, determine the success of the adoption.

If a company sees a need to do things better and decides to adopt the Scanlon Plan or is considering its adoption, how can it proceed so that the chances for a successful installation are improved? Even if the company hires a consultant who knows the plan, it will need to answer major questions and explore many aspects of its operations. More than likely, the company and consultant will develop and explore a check list with these items.

1. Who knows what about the plan and the company and what are the expectations about the plan's success in the company?

2. What is the human relations climate within the managerial group, within the nonmanagerial group, and between the two groups?
3. What are the problems and procedures in structuring and establishing the Participation System?
4. What are the problems and procedures in structuring and establishing the Equity System?
5. How can the organization review the plan to see if it is working, how often should it be done and by whom?

WHO KNOWS WHAT?

If a company undertakes to install a Scanlon Plan, all people within the company must cooperate to improve productivity with the expectation that successful cooperation will produce bonuses. If information about the company and the plan and expectations about the operation of the plan within the company are unrealistic, chances of success are small. A central question to explore is who knows what about the plan and the company and what are their expectations about how the plan will work in the particular organization?

To be informed about the company means that a person sees a need to do some things better, but is at the same time aware of the organization's strengths. People throughout the organization need to be generally aware of, and in general agreement about, the problems that exist. Likewise, people need to have information about the potentials to meet these problems. If the company has problems and at the same time has indifferent leadership, outdated technical skills and capacities, inadequate resources, and uninterested and incompetent people, then the problems are likely to persist. If the skills, abilities, resources, interests, and competencies are in the company, the problems are more likely to be solved.

People need to see reasons for change and the potentials for improving. People also need information about the Scanlon Plan. Are the basic ideas of cooperation, participation, and equity generally well understood? Is there awareness among people at all levels of the organization that they must share information, skills, and ideas that until now may have been considered proprietary and secret? Does each individual recognize that he/she may need to change his/her behavior. Is there awareness that the installation of the plan is not inviting Santa Claus in to give you a present, but is more like inviting in a trusted friend to work with you on a hard job?

Expectations about success depend on knowledge of both the company and the plan and on a judgment about how well the needs for change are

18

likely to be met by initiating the plan. A simplified version of this process of determining who knows what would be to locate all members of the organization on a set of axes such as those in Table 2, which classifies people as informed opposers, informed supporters, intuitive opposers, or intuitive supporters, Obviously, these are artificial categories. In any real situation, there may be genuine neutrals, mild supporters, partially informed people, and so forth.

If all people are in the top right quadrant, then the company should go ahead with the plan, since everyone knows the company and the plan and expects success. If all members of the company are in the bottom half of the figure, then the need is to seek more information about the company and the plan. Each company will present its own picture and about the only thing that the pictures will have in common is that people will not be concentrated in one quadrant but will appear in all areas. The particular pattern must be examined and used as one of the bases for deciding to adopt the plan, to not adopt the plan, or to gather more information.

Various possibilities are almost infinite; however, a few examples may illustrate the value of exploring who knows what in the company.

If most management people are intuitive supporters and most nonmanagement people are intuitive opposers, then the plan should not be started. It should either be dropped altogether, or members of the organization should attempt to get the required information or develop the required skills, resources, and so forth. One likely step is for management to begin to develop and communicate a better definition of the company, its problems and promises, its deficits and potentials. Additional information may also come from contacts with companies that have the plan, from consultants, from reading, or from other available educational sources.

If a key person or group—for example, the president of the company or

TABLE 2

Classification of People Based on Their Information and Expectations

		Expectations about the plan	
		It will not work	It will work
Information about the company and the plan	Much about both	Informed opposers	Informed supporters
	Little about either	Intuitive opposers	Intuitive supporters

of the union, or the executive committee of the union or of the company —is in the informed opposers' quadrant, the plan should be dropped from consideration at this time. No matter how the rest of the organization may try to cooperate, the key person or group is very likely to thwart success.

If the total organization, including the key people and groups, is well informed but evenly divided on expectations, then the plan should be dropped from consideration or delayed until the conflict is resolved. In this situation, adopting the plan for a definite trial period with an evaluation plan jointly developed by opposers and supporters may be a way of resolving the problem.

Determining who knows what can take more or less time depending on obvious features such as size, complexity, and number of locations of the company. It will also depend on the number of people assigned to the task and their ability to obtain this kind of information from members of the company. A consultant trained to obtain and interpret large amounts of complex data may be very useful. Haphazard interviews or attitude surveys may be harmful to the company and very likely work against a Scanlon Plan working well even if initiated.

The intention of determining who knows what is to be as clear as possible about the risks which the company is taking if it does move to a Scanlon Plan. Table 2 shows a way of representing one basis for the company's decision. The decision belongs to the company and will be influenced not only by the information but by what risks can be tolerated by whom.

WHAT IS THE CLIMATE?

A somewhat different information dimension, but one closely related to who knows what, is the human climate of the company, or as it is frequently called the industrial relations climate. Do the relations among people seem to be consistent with the basic values of the plan? Are relations marked by trust, confidence in people's abilities, regard for people, ability to deal with conflict, cooperation, and participation in all areas and aspects of the company? If so, the climate is favorable to the growth of the plan. In all areas and aspects, the climate will seldom be totally favorable or unfavorable. What is likely is that the climate will be uncertain, and the decision-making processes of the company will need to judge climate as one more information base.

Assessing the climate requires that the range of opinion and the modal opinion of at least two major groups be obtained and compared. How does

TABLE 3
Human Relations Climate Groups

Management	Nonmanagement	
	Union	Nonunion
Top management	Leadership	Staff, professional, sales, other similar groups
Middle management	Membership	
Lower management		

management (first-line supervisors and above) see industrial relations within the organization, and how does nonmanagement see these relations? These evaluations concentrate on the past and present levels of trust, confidence, regard, cooperation, conflict management, and participation, but also try to obtain forecasts. A situation in which things are bad and getting worse is quite different from one in which the climate is bad but getting better. Along with the assessment of people's perceptions and opinions, a review of company policy and practice is a vital part of determining the climate.

If there is a union in the company, then an obvious place to look is at past and present union-management relations, formal and informal, and at the products of the relation, for example, contracts, and policies. Also valuable is the comparison of perceptions and attitudes of union leadership, union membership, and nonunion, nonmanagerial groups—for example, accounting staff—to see what similarities and differences there are within each of the groups and between the groups. In a parallel fashion, a comparison of the perceptions of different levels of management is highly valuable.

If there is no union, there is not likely to be a formal history of employee-management relations, that is, no contracts or written agreements. Likewise personnel policies and practices are likely to show that they were formulated on management's perceptions about employees rather than on actual inputs from employees. Instead of being able to look for trust and the other attributes in the *formal* relationship, the examination needs to examine the more casual and informal relationships and the strictly on-the-job, employee-management contacts. In this case, the valuable comparisons of nonmanagement people can be obtained by examining similarities and differences within each department—for example, the finishing department or the clerical pool—and between the different departments. Comparisons of middle and lower managers in different departments will also be valuable.

Table 3 represents the importance for establishing the human relations climate of comparing similarities and differences between the management and nonmanagement groups. The table also emphasizes the importance of looking at the range of opinion within the major groups and the value of comparing any differences of opinion among the subgroups of the major groups.

PROBLEMS AND PROCEDURES IN ESTABLISHING THE PARTICIPATION SYSTEM

In establishing this system, the company needs to consider the exact structure of the system and the content of the system.

The number of Production Committees depends on the number of supervised units of the company. The company needs to be very clear about its own structure to insure that every employee is represented in the system. Does each shift of a department need a committee? If a foreman has two leadmen should there be one or two Production Committees in that department? Should a department of forty and a department of six each have one elected representative? For the Screening Committee, there will be questions of who the management representatives should be and how many elected representatives there should be. To provide representative structure for both committees, the election procedures and frequency of elections should be clearly specified.

Information about productivity and information about the bonus are the two kinds of content of the Participation System. Some difficulties may arise in specifying the difference between a suggestion and a grievance or complaint or in emphasizing that suggestions must meet the two standards of economic merit and feasibility to be accepted. However, the major problems are with the financial content of the system. Financial data are treated with great secrecy in many companies, and the idea of communicating sales figures, labor costs, and the other bonus-related data to everyone in the organization may cause great stress. Members of management may feel that people should not have such information, that they do not understand such information, that a competitor will gain access to the information and gain an advantage, or that, for other reasons, "It is just not a good idea to trust people that far." Other employees may feel that they do not need to know the information, that management is trying to confuse them, or that, for other reasons, "It is not a good idea to trust management to get it straight."

Developing the content of a monthly financial report to all employees may be a critical point in getting started with the Scanlon Plan. What estimates of employee knowledge, ability to learn, and trustworthiness are made in determining how much and what kinds of financial information are to be communicated and shared may be the central question in determining the climate and information-expectation level of the company.

PROBLEMS AND PROCEDURES IN ESTABLISHING THE EQUITY SYSTEM

To establish the Equity System, a company needs to do specifically what was discussed in a general way in the previous section: it must develop its own specific *ratio* and *bonus plan*. Knowledge of accountancy and knowledge of the recent history and present operations of the company are the major requirements for this task, and an equitable, understandable, acceptable, and accurate representation of the organization's present level of productivity is the goal.

Collecting salary, wage, and benefit information may pose some problems, but is usually a relatively easy task. Problems may arise from the secrecy surrounding the compensation of executives. Other problems will occasionally arise about benefits. How should vacation pay be handled, sick pay, holiday pay? Are the costs of the retirees' picnic to be included? How? How about the company's gift to employees at the end of the year and the bowling and softball teams that the company sponsors? These and related problems must be solved. However, the major problem related to personnel costs will be that some people will not want everyone to be included. The president or the executive committee may feel that they should be excluded because "It is not fair to have annual salary and hourly hired people get the same bonus. If they improve productivity, let them get all the bonus." Many production workers may agree with the president's argument. If it is true that the president cannot facilitate productivity improvement, then the company does indeed have a serious problem! If it is not true, then the necessity of cooperation needs to be expressed in the determination of the ratio. Similar arguments may develop about other groups of employees, for example, the clerical pool, janitors, research and design engineers.

A problem that relates to the month-by-month computation of the ratio and the distribution of the bonus is the status of the newly hired. How long should a person be with the company before he becomes eligible for a bonus?

23

Normally a period of thirty, sixty, or ninety days is used as the answer. Longer or shorter periods may make more sense in a particular situation. It is even possible to develop a plan whereby employees get increasingly larger shares of a full bonus as they stay with the company. In any case, there is an incentive to help newcomers learn quickly so that they pull their own weight.

The second part of the ratio, developing the value of production, especially on a month at a time basis, is typically the more difficult part of establishing the Equity System. The basic problems can be approached by referring to a general formula.

Value of production = value of finished goods sold adjusted for
1. changes in finished and in-process inventory
2. goods returned for reasons of poor quality.

A general problem may arise if the present accounting system and manpower cannot generate the information needed to compute monthly bonuses at a suitable rate of speed. In that case, a decision about changing the system or hiring new people will be required before proceeding with the plan. Specific problems may arise as to when to value goods sold—at shipment, on receipt by purchaser, or on payment for goods. Adjustments to the sales value may be a problem. How shall finished inventory be valued, at sales price or production cost? Should adjustments be made on the basis of changes in the value of goods in process before finished inventory? Is it fair to adjust for returned goods? Should the value of returned goods be subtracted from current values when the "mistake" was made weeks or months earlier?

In putting the initial ratio together and thinking about how it will operate in the months ahead, other questions will arise about the influence of capital investment, or changes in wages, prices, and product mix. All parties should know that changes in the ratio should be discussed when major changes occur in operations. However, all parties should be equally clear that the ratio is not subject to month-to-month tinkering.

After the ratio and the procedures for determining it each month are set, there are still two key decisions to be made. How are the gains from productivity improvement to be divided between company and employees? What percentage of the bonus pool should be put in contingency reserve to protect the equity of the company? The answer to the first question depends on the current financial position of the company and on the risks the board of directors and management are willing to take. A company that is just breaking even may require a substantial share of the improvement in order to accelerate organizational improvement. A company with good profits may feel that taking no share and relying on better management of other resources may be the best path. The answer to the second question depends most significantly on the nature of the business cycle of the company. Erratic patterns of sales indicate a need for large reserves, while consistent sales patterns indicate that small reserves will be adequate. Again the important point is that the division must be accepted at the beginning by the participants.

REVIEWING THE PLAN

An integral part of getting started with a plan is to be clear about what "it" is supposed to help the parties accomplish. Along with specifying the goals of a plan goes the need to establish methods and standards for reviewing and evaluating its operation.

When a plan works, each of the systems works. The Participation System leads to productivity improvement by generating many, good quality ideas. The Equity System pays off in higher income for all members of the organization. In addition to these more tangible measures, the organization expects to improve in its people relations. Trust, confidence, regard for people, cooperation, conflict management, and participation are expected to improve. The operation of a plan is under continuous review, and once each month the Screening Committee report indicates the status of suggestions and bonus. Since all members of the company have access to the report, all members are reviewing and evaluating the plan. The number of suggestions, the areas from which suggestions come, the problems addressed by the suggestions and the ratio of accepted to rejected suggestions all become standards for reviewing the system. The number and size of bonuses become ways of evaluating that system. The increased understanding of the bonus computation provides a review. Each person can keep track of his own attitudes about the company on the dimensions of trust and so forth and can check with others in his work group to see what they are thinking.

A major review of the plan is held once a year. At this time the total pattern of suggestions and bonuses gives information about the success or shortcomings of the plan. The size of the contingency reserve fund becomes one very significant measure. The matter of improvement in human relations or greater commitment to the basic philosophy are more difficult to arrive at. If a systematic review of attitudes and opinions is done before the

25

plan is initiated, then a similar review once a year can provide answers. Other measures such as absenteeism and turnover may provide indirect answers.

If the organization has worked with a consultant in the early stages of considering the plan and during the first year of operation, the consultant may be valuable as an objective outsider. If he was instrumental in assessing the original people climate, he will be valuable in assessing any changes that have occurred.

Most important of all is to see if the total company in all its activities is improving. The central goal is not to have the plan work but to have the company improve. If bonuses are high and frequent, if suggestions are plentiful, and if all the people in the organization feel very good, but the company is going deeper and deeper into the red, the plan is not working well.

Summary

The Scanlon Plan is an abstraction. At the most general level, it is a philosophy of human nature and human relations from which is derived a theory of organization which emphasizes participation by more people in more activities of the organization and a set of management principles for encouraging the expression of human potential. In the concrete applications of the plan two kinds of mechanisms are emphasized. One set of mechanisms, the Participation System, encourages people to think about their jobs and make suggestions for improving them and thus increase organization-wide productivity. There is also a way to provide equitable compensation to all members of the organization based on better corporate performance through the ratio and the bonus mechanisms of the Equity System. No two concrete applications of the abstraction are the same.

In the next chapter the emphasis will turn from the mechanics of the plan to a fuller account of the intentions of the plan and what it accomplishes when it works well.

CHAPTER 2

Purposes
and Assumptions

EARLY APPLICATIONS of the Scanlon Plan tried to improve cooperation between union and management and to improve the economic equity between the employees and the total organization. The mechanisms for accomplishing these purposes were not taken from a particular theory of organization, management, or human relations. Instead, they were a collection of procedures and ideas about how an incentive system might work, how to communicate within the company in order to accomplish the purposes of equity and participation, how committees might aid cooperation, and how better decisions might be made. Scanlon saw his activities growing not from a theoretical position but from a firm belief in the worth of the human individual and the individual's capacity for growth and his ability to contribute with head as well as hands to the success of the work organization. The essence of the plan was to implement, within a company, mechanisms that were specially suited to its particular technology and problems and that would capitalize on the individual's capacity for growth and ability to contribute.

For many years, Scanlon Plan applications, especially the successes, were activities looking for an explanation and for theoretical support. They gave the appearance of bridges constructed by a primitive tribe, with no formal knowledge of the theory of physics or engineering, but "the bridges", nevertheless, connected two points, bore the load, and did the job. Today the purposes and assumptions of the plan are more explicit. Case studies and research in the broad areas of union-management relations, human relations, and organization change have contributed to a detailing of the purposes and assumptions of the plan. A large body of old and new research about the Scanlon Plan is reviewed in Chapters 6 and 7. However, at this point the general findings of research in these areas are presented as background and support for the current statement of purposes and assumptions of the plan.

UNION-MANAGEMENT RELATIONS

At one time Scanlon himself thought that the plan could not succeed without an employee union. Acceptance of this assumption led to skepticism on the part of management, especially those whose companies had weak unions and were not interested in strengthening them or those whose companies which neither had nor wanted a union. On the other hand, unions were sometimes skeptical of the plan because they felt that cooperation might weaken the employees' commitment to the purposes of the union.

Individual cases showed Scanlon that he was wrong. Today companies with and without unions are operating successfully with the plan. In some companies adoption of the plan has weakened the union, and in others it has strengthened the union. There are cases where the plan was dropped after a union was voted in. The existence of the plan within a company does not necessarily weaken or strengthen the union.

Whether there is a union or not, cooperation between managerial and nonmanagerial people is vital to the success of a company and its Scanlon Plan. Cooperation is vital, since there are real differences between management and nonmanagement, and these differences need to be resolved. A union to represent the nonmanagement people is not necessary. However, if a union does exist, the differences between the management and nonmanagement groups are more likely to have been defined and clarified by collective bargaining procedures, and the specific requirements for cooperation are probably clearer. If a union exists, especially if it has good leadership and is strong, then union support of the plan is essential to its success. If a company has no union or a weak union and the managerial and nonmanagerial differences are not clearly defined, the mechanisms of the plan

28

may help define the differences, either by strengthening the union or by developing other means through the Participation System.

The purpose in adopting the plan should not be to develop "one big happy family where there are no differences." It should be to try to make the differences that exist clear to both parties and to create mechanisms and a climate that resolve the differences in a cooperative manner based on common goals. A suggestion from a lathe operator is inherently a disagreement with management about how to do the job. While the Scanlon Plan is neither pro- nor anti-union, it has been generally successful in improving union-management relations. However, it is not restricted to that context, but operates in the broader context of human relations and the use of human resources in the organization.

HUMAN RELATIONS AND HUMAN RESOURCES

In the past twenty-five to thirty years, research in human relations and human resources has grown in volume and in quality. From some early ideas about the importance of relatively superficial ways in which people in organizations relate to each other, research has moved steadily toward dealing with deeper and more complex issues concerning people in organizations, how they relate to each other, how they relate to their work and their jobs, and how they relate to the goals and demands of the organization.

This research about people working in organizations has contributed to our improved knowledge of how the plan works. Particularly important is the work on leadership and an accompanying emphasis on supervisory and managerial training. A major finding of leadership research has been that no particular physical or psychological characteristics can guarantee that a person will be an effective leader. Effective leadership depends on the behavior of the leader, his relationship to the group he is leading, and the total organizational context in which the behavior is occurring. Effective leadership is situation-specific. These findings have produced an emphasis on two general kinds of "leadership" training. One kind seeks to improve leadership within a specific situation by helping the individual manager-supervisor understand his company, his group, and himself better. Another kind seeks to broaden the individual as a leader by helping him know the varieties of groups and individuals, the varieties of organizations, and the varieties of responses which his behavior may elicit from the various situations in which he may find himself as leader. All this training has empha-

29

sized that leaders need to know the findings of the sciences that deal with people and their ways of interacting.

Much of the content of management-development instruction has been provided by the increasing body of theory and information derived from research by those interested in human relations in the work setting. A later chapter will explore some of these findings in more detail. In general, what has emerged are new understandings about what motivates people in the work place. Older notions about the primacy of financial reward in motivating people have been challenged and reformulated within a broader view of the nature of man. Money and financial reward are important to motivation, but so too are opportunities to satisfy other human needs related to desires for high regard from fellow workers, for status as an individual, for understanding the job to be done, and for meaning (importance) in the work to be done.

Historically, the guiding thesis in human relations research has been that treating people better makes them happier and that happier people are more productive in accomplishing the goals of the organization. Much time has been devoted to defining what each of the words in the thesis means and to clarifying the basic notion of "happy means productive." While the thesis is confirmed in some situations, it is clear that it is *not* a general law, with obvious ways of being applied across all situations. Some unhappy people are very productive; perhaps more damning to the "happy-means-productive" idea, there are people who are happy in the work place and unproductive, or at best minimally productive.

A variation of the thesis is that even if happy people are not more productive, the well-being of members of an organization is a goal which should be pursued for its own sake. In line with this variation, several notions about the trade-offs between productivity and individual well-being have been suggested. For example, while present well-being may mean lower productivity, it insures that individuals will stay with the organization and thus make long-term productivity more likely. Unfortunately, for this point of view, people differ on how important productivity is to immediate and long-term well-being. As an example, the company president's well-being, mental health, and happiness may depend closely on immediate productivity. This fact may put him in direct conflict with people who want to participate in company affairs even at the cost of reducing immediate productivity. The idea that the president should sacrifice his personal well-being for "the future good of the organization" may not seem to the president to be a compelling argument. Likewise, asking a secretary to take a pay cut for "the good of the company" may not seem like a good idea to her.

A second variation of the thesis is that, since happy people *can* be productive (and productive people *can* be happy), we *ought* to operate our organizations so that it is true. The difficulty with this position is that some people say we *ought not*. A further difficulty is that we cannot say that *all* individuals can be productive and happy. It is possible that some people, and maybe many people, cannot be both.

The actual state of the art and science at this time is that treating people "better," according to what they consider to be better, *can* produce "happier" people, and "happier" people *can* be more productive in obtaining organizational goals. *But,* such is not always the case.

The Scanlon Plan activities, especially the committee activities and the election procedures, emphasize leadership training, participation, and motivation throughout the organization. Management and nonmanagement people have an opportunity to learn more about the different kinds and qualities of leadership, participation, and motivation that exist in the company, in particular work groups, and in particular people. Many people have an opportunity to be leaders and learn that leading is more than commanding, demanding, and deciding. Many people can test in their own experience how different ways of relating to people affect productivity in the organization.

ORGANIZATION CHANGE

Research about organizations and how to change them has shown that even though organizations are complex, they are entities that exist in time and space and can be changed in a controlled manner. Organizations are not accidents, nor are they restricted to reacting to events in their environments. This same research has emphasized the need to consider simultaneously the structure, the technology, the processes of leadership, communication, and authority, and the human relations climate in order to really understand an organization. Further, it has indicated that understanding must precede successful planned change.

An organization is people cooperating to accomplish things that one person could not do alone. Much research is concerned with how to get people to cooperate, the effects of the manner of obtaining cooperation, and how to insure that cooperation promotes the organization's goals. Other research is concerned with how organizations go about determining what they should do. What this research has shown is that organizations can become more effective by encouraging all members to participate (each in his own way) in establishing goals, in planning to reach goals, and in taking action to implement the plans. Again, the generality of this research is uncertain. The possible positive effects of participation have been demonstrated but not proven (see Chapter 6). The Scanlon Plan encourages participation and provides a way of assessing its effects.

Purposes

Now after thirty years of application, demonstration, and research input, the purposes of the Scanlon Plan are broader and at the same time more specific. The purposes of applying the Scanlon Plan are to develop a more effective organization and more effective people within the organization.

EFFECTIVENESS

At a general level, the same definition of effectiveness can be applied to organizations or to individuals. Effectiveness is a measure of the extent to which the organization or individual has the kinds of effects on the environment—natural, technical, social—that it wants to.[1] Likewise, for both the organization and the individual, effectiveness has a present and a future dimension.

For the organization, effectiveness means maximizing or optimizing present productivity and surviving to insure future productivity. Any activity that improves present productivity and enhances the likelihood that the organization will continue to exist in the future is a positive developmental change. However, a particular activity, action, or event may have dissimilar effects on present productivity and survival. Table 4 illustrates a way of classifying the impact of an activity on organization effectiveness.

If an activity increases productivity and survival value or increases one dimension without influencing the other, then the activity is effective. If an activity decreases both dimensions or decreases one without influencing the other, then the activity is ineffective.

For the two corners designated by "?," the cases in which an activity has opposite effects on the two dimensions, one cannot determine a general classification. Activities that fall in these areas can be judged on effectiveness only by reference to the specifics of the organization and its situation.

32

TABLE 4
Impact of an Activity on Organization Effectiveness

Survival Value	Present Productivity		
	Increase	Same	Decrease
Increase	effective	effective	?
Same	effective	trivial	ineffective
Decrease	?	ineffective	ineffective

Suppose a company is about to start a training program for newly hired people. Based on staff reports, it is clear that using production operations to train these people will lessen present productivity but can reasonably be expected to improve survival value by reducing total training costs over a period of time. This situation is shown in the top right-hand corner of Table 4. Is the activity effective or ineffective? The answer requires details that can be obtained only from the real situation: how many people are to be trained, how long a period does it take to amortize the training costs, do the trained workers see the program as stupid because they see only the immediate impact, what recent events have occurred which have affected the trust relationship between the training staff group and the other employees?

An example from the bottom left-hand corner of Table 4 would be to keep the machine room running this afternoon instead of shutting it down for a maintenance check. By running, we are likely to look better today, but how does skipping the maintenance check jeopardize future operations? Again the need is for here-and-now details, not theoretical solutions. Can we shut down tomorrow? Are we talking about a shutdown at the beginning, middle, or end of a stock run? Is there any information concerning machine operation within the last two weeks that suggests a problem? Are the people running the machines willing to take the risk?

Effectiveness for an individual within a particular group also has an immediate and a future component. The effective individual is productive by making efficient and satisfying use of his skills, abilities, characteristics —of himself. He also expects that his present actions are taking him toward goals he prefers. If he is effective now, he may look forward to being an effective person with the organization for a longer time. The individual does, of course, have an existence apart from the organization, and he can survive even if the organization fails. He is interested in his total effectiveness as a person which is different from, but no doubt related to, his more limited

33

effectiveness with a particular organization. If he is not effective now, efficient and satisfied now, with this company he will go elsewhere if he can. Effectiveness for the individual is mainly concerned with the present, though his expectations do make him aware of the future.

Table 5 represents the two dimensions of individual effectiveness: present productivity and present satisfaction with the content and context of the job. Using this table, it is possible to determine the effect of an activity on individual effectiveness. Any event or activity which improves the individual's productivity and satisfaction makes the person more effective in this particular organization.

In general, a good present condition of effectiveness predicts a good future, and people probably *expect* to stay with the organization. Similarly, actions that make people less effective predict that people will leave the organization. Of course, people may do "irrational" things; and some percentage of effective people will leave, and ineffective people will stay. In two segments of table 5, expectation probably plays the deciding role in classifying an event or action as effective or otherwise, In the top right-hand segment would be the case of Theresa, who has just been promoted from the clerical pool to a receptionist job. The promotion enhances her satisfaction but reduces her present productivity because she needs to learn new skills of telephone use and meeting the public and can no longer rely completely on her well-practiced skills of typing and filing. Theresa's expectations about how fast and how well she can fit into the new job are two of the crucial pieces of information needed to accurately classify the promotion as making Theresa a more or less effective person and member of this organization. In the bottom left-hand segment, we might find the case of Darlene, an assistant supervisor at Jerd's Tool Company, who has just completed a supervisors' training program. Her productivity is greater, she is better at her job, and her satisfaction may be greater if she wishes to excel as an assistant supervisor. However, her satisfaction may be less if she

TABLE 5
Impact of an Activity on Individual Effectiveness

Present satisfaction with job content and context	Present Productivity		
	Increase	Same	Decrease
Increase	effective	effective	?
Same	effective	trivial	ineffective
Decrease	?	ineffective	ineffective

thinks she should be promoted to supervisor. The impact of the training on Darlene depends on her desire to be promoted and on her expectations about being promoted—whether she will be promoted and when. To illustrate again the difference between total-person effectiveness and effectiveness in a particular organization, consider what Darlene may do. She may take a supervisor position in another company, an action that may increase her personal effectiveness but reduces her effectiveness at Jerd's Tool Company to zero. As with the description of organization effectiveness, there are no ways to give general answers for the two corner segments. Classification is specific to the situation.

The Scanlon Plan is intended to improve organization productivity and survival and each individual's productivity and satisfaction within the organization. Further, through the mechanisms and emphasis on participation and communication the plan provides ways to handle activities and events that may have opposite effects on present and future productivity or opposite effects on employee productivity and satisfaction. The Scanlon Plan mechanisms provide ways of resolving conflict and dealing with actions which are of uncertain usefulness for increasing the effectiveness of the individual or of the organization.

Developing more effective organizations and more effective individuals means change.

CHANGE

Implementing the Scanlon Plan means that the organization and its people must be prepared to deal with two kinds of change—planned and unplanned. Planned change refers to a process of identifying problems in the organization, proposing actions to solve the problems (for example, a new accounting system, a restructuring of the organization, or a new piece of equipment), and putting the plan into action. For an individual in the organization, it may mean setting an objective, establishing a way of, as well as a timetable for, attaining the objective and putting the plan into action. Unplanned change refers to events that happen outside the area of organization control or expectation, which create problems for the organization or require new actions immediately. For example, a competitor develops a new technique, taxes are raised, the average education level of line workers increases by two school years. Theoretically, the organization may have control of an area; but if, in fact, the organization does not have a plan for dealing with an event, it is facing an unplanned change.

Frequently, the difference between planned and unplanned change refers to the amount of time available for "planning" and to the number of options available. Planned change usually implies longer time periods to identify and react to problems and more options for meeting the problems. An extreme example of unplanned change would be lightning striking a plant and setting it ablaze; here the time period is very short, and the options are to put out the fire or to let it burn. A planned change is not a surprise; an unplanned change is.

Distinguishing sharply between planned and unplanned change is difficult for a total organization. The distinction is less difficult to make for an individual. For an individual, the distinction hinges on whether he is consciously trying to bring about a change in himself or his environment, or is reacting to a change in his circumstance. The same basic difference applies to an organization; but since an organization is made up of people with different information, attitudes, characteristics, and perceptions of "reality," what may appear as a planned change to one individual or group may be an unplanned change to others in the same organization. A new cost accounting procedure which is carefully planned by top management and the financial people and has a good chance of solving a problem within the company may seem to the line supervisor to be a sudden change in his circumstances to which he must react without a specific plan.

PROBLEMS OF CHANGE

The problem of change is not in getting changes but in attempting to reduce negative reaction to unplanned and *perceived* unplanned change and in assuring that changes move the organization in the right direction, at the right speed, at the right time.

Getting change is no problem. Anyone can change an organization. Anyone can go into a factory and say to the first ten people he meets, "It is not true that this operation will be moved to Idaho (or Ohio if the factory is in Idaho)." Change will occur, and probably before he gets to the tenth person. If you own a factory, hire a hundred people tomorrow and fire them next Wednesday. If you do not own a factory, but just work there, get a large, closed packing case and put it in a corner of your work area with a large sign saying TO BE OPENED OCTOBER 20. Or if you want to get a key executive to change his behavior, kick him in the shinbone or say to him twice a day for the next week, "You are the most trustworthy man I've ever met."

Even if no one in particular is trying to change the organization, change will occur. With time, the work force will get older, become better educated, become younger, include more women or more blacks, or change on any one or more of scores of dimensions. An organization may stop selling pigeons to be sacrificed in the temple, may start making neckties that glow in the dark, may be unionized, may have taxes raised, may cease to exist.

The problem is not getting change but controlling change when it is undertaken as a matter of choice or making the best preparation when change is imposed from outside the organization. Both controlling and reacting to change depend on relating the actions taken to the various goals of increased effectiveness. In a particular company, the relation of action to effectiveness is not an abstract exercise in taxonomy; it is a real and immediate problem.

The Scanlon Plan rests on certain assumptions about how to meet the problem of change in a specific organization. The assumptions are of two sorts. There are some fairly specific assumptions about how to meet problems of change in the organization. These are discussed in the next section. There are also what might be called strategy assumptions that deal with the best ways to initiate and maintain the Scanlon Plan as an instrument of organization development. These are discussed in a later section.

Assumptions About Organization Development

The basic assumptions about organization development which are consistent with the way the Scanlon Plan has evolved are that:

1. Development requires that there be explicit conscious activity and planning to become more effective and to make more effective reactions to imposed changes.

2. The improvement of individuals and organizations begins with effective activity in the present situation.

3. Broad participation, rather than restrictive participation, provides a better definition of the present situation and provides a better base for effective activity.

4. Establishing organization processes for defining the present situation, solving problems, resolving conflict, and improving effectiveness is no less, and probably more, important to an organization's development than specifying particular end goals for the company.

5. Frequent evaluation of the change process is necessary to establish the value of the mechanisms of change and of the organization's progress toward improved effectiveness.

37

Organizations need to establish an overall framework for the meaning of change so that members of the organization understand that planning for change and reacting to changes are related activities that enhance effectiveness. The Equity and Participation systems of the Scanlon Plan provide this framework. Each suggestion of change is assessed to see if it is likely to improve the immediate payroll/sales relationship and thus generate a bonus and enhance survival. The assessment involves: (1) will it improve productivity; (2) is it feasible at this time? The Equity and Participation systems encourage and enable everyone in the organization to think about change, to see the bases for evaluating change, and offers everyone practice in generating and reacting to change. Given learning time, a variety of changes, and practice with the systems people can develop a rational attitude toward change, that is, change can lead to improvement but let us check *this one* to see if it will.

START WHERE YOU ARE

This assumption emphasizes two parts: doing, and doing it in the context of the actual problem. Changing, becoming more effective, requires practice, and practice means doing. A frequent problem in the early stages of Scanlon Plan activity is that in Screening Committee meetings elected members do not talk. If elected representatives continue to be quiet, the Scanlon Plan has no chance of working. The problem must be dealt with immediately by management and by the elected representatives. Management must do—they must try to encourage discussion; and the elected representatives must do—they must say something. Eventually, this group may discuss and develop the master plan for the company's next five years, but it will not do so if it is not able to solve the present problem.

When an individual or a group deals with a present problem, previous experience and assumptions about the future are important considerations. They are important, though, only to the extent that they are available and perceived to be important to the present situation (relevant). If no one in a group knows that the cube root of 27 is 3, or if no one in the group mentions it, then that information is not part of the present situation. Likewise, if a group is unanimous in expecting the Tigers to win the pennant, but no one can connect this consensus with decreased line speed, then it is not part of the present situation.

In a particular situation, when an individual or group is attempting to define the present and "suspects" that something else is needed that is not immediately perceived to be available or relevant, then time is spent doing research, for example, a long-term laboratory experiment or a short five minutes of general discussion. Usually, in an organization action regarding a problem is required within certain time and resource constraints so that judgments need to be made about how much time-resource can be spent on research for the present problem.

INVOLVE EVERYONE

As demonstrated in both the Participation and the Equity systems, the Scanlon Plan assumes that broad participation is better than narrow. Relating this assumption to the one above, we would say that present action is most likely to be effective when parties to the action agree on a definition of the present situation. If conflict arises about what the present problem is, then time must be spent arriving at a common definition of the present reality *before* attempting to deal with any conflict about alternative solutions. If agreement exists about what the problem is, then the possible solutions are likely to be few rather than many and consensus *should be* easier to establish. Multiple solutions imply multiple problems, that is, disagreement about what the present situation really is.

Practical constraints of time, money, or energy may require that actions be taken even with disagreement about the nature of the present situation. In this circumstance, the assumption is that the eventual solution will be better, and more widely accepted, because the participants recognize the tentative nature of the proposed solution, the risks involved in taking action, and the likelihood of dealing with the problem on a continuing basis.

Another possibility is that of genuine disagreement about solutions even with consensus about the problem. In this circumstance, conflict is a part of the situation and is dealt with openly in taking actions toward a solution.

The questions of who should participate in what kinds of organizational decisions and activities are answered pragmatically, situation by situation and problem by problem, but with the idea that people learn.

Participation by many rather than few increases the likelihood that more of the salient and relevant materials will be included in the definition of the present situation. As groups work together over time, they will test the accuracy, saliency, and relevance of material contributed by various members and will establish consensus on who should participate in what. Participation likewise increases the likelihood that the direction, speed, and timing

39

of change are appropriate. Generally, reducing the surprise and threat of change by involving more people can increase commitment to change and insure that change is accomplished at a lower cost to the organization and the individual.

The only absolute in the Scanlon Plan regarding participation is that everyone participates in receiving, or not receiving a bonus. Participation by offering suggestions, voting in elections, or serving as an elected representative on committees is encouraged but not demanded.

SETUP PROCESS

The Scanlon Plan activities are based on an assumption that the key to organization development is to establish a process that relates and, if possible, involves everyone in the present condition of the organization. The process encourages people to propose changes and to evaluate them on their payroll/sales effectiveness, and compensates people for improving the organization. The compensation goes to those who are active in proposing and evaluating changes and also goes to those who accept and carry out the changes others propose. Compensation for those who are not active is justified in two general ways. Those who are not active now may become so and "pay back" their fellow workers in the future. Also facilitating or permitting change, rather than blocking it, is considered a positive contribution.

The process is open to all, and all are encouraged by the words and deeds of those who work with them, as well as by tangible compensation, to participate in changing the organization to make it more productive. The direction of change is improvement of the present condition, and the general goal is increased effectiveness. No highly abstract end states are set as goals, since such goals may be difficult for many people in the company to understand, difficult to translate into specific behavior, and present no concrete paths from the present point in time to the time they are supposed to be achieved.

Each person examines his own job and suggests changes. In this way, the range of change is directly related to the range of jobs in the organization. People whose work has immediate results and people who must use projections about future results can all propose ways to make themselves and the total organization more effective. Thus, while the process is largely one of taking care of today and worrying about tomorrow tomorrow, it is not exclusively that. Rather the actual importance of tomorrow to the particular company is weighted by the number and kinds of people who must deal with tomorrow in their day-to-day activities. For example, increasing today's production is the immediate concern of many but it must be related to the best possible information about what demand there will be for the product in tomorrow's market.

The process is also a vehicle for on-the-job training in the specifics of human relations and their quality and importance in the operations of the organization. The original assumptions of the Scanlon Plan about the advantages of cooperation, participation, trust, and authentic behavior have received general support from the research of the past several years. Nevertheless, the state of knowledge does not permit specific prescriptions for obtaining these conditions in a company nor for the specific form the advantages may take. The Scanlon Plan process provides a context in which the particular people in a particular company can determine how to obtain the conditions and what forms the advantages can take. Just as learning about the company's operations takes place in small, incremental steps, based on present problems and the value of productivity, so too does learning about human relations. Learning about real problems, real people, real relationships, and real productivity becomes an integral part of the job. Those who learn best, most, and fastest can make greater contributions to the organization and their own effectiveness. The continuing emphasis on learning provides an atmosphere in which all people *can* learn no matter what their speed and power as learners and no matter how many "wrong" lessons may need to be unlearned.

Key elements of the process are the Equity and Participation systems. These mechanisms permit and encourage learning, change, and improvement in the areas of operations and human relations. Using these mechanisms, the organization, through its individual members, identifies problems, defines the context of the problem, proposes solutions, evaluates the solutions, resolves conflicts about both the problem and the solutions, and provides information and compensation as feedback concerning the process.

EVALUATE OFTEN

Evaluation of the Scanlon Plan has been discussed in the first chapter as a central part of the process of getting started. From the assumptions presented, it should be clear that the Scanlon Plan is always getting started in a company. The mechanisms and the total process are constantly dealing with new problems, new technologies, new findings from the human relations and other research areas, people who have changed and new people who bring various kinds and levels of skills, abilities, attitudes, and ideas to the organization. The process of improving effectiveness is continuous, and so too is the evaluation. Each suggestion, each meeting, each bonus period, each year-end appraisal is part of the evaluation. Criteria for evaluation range from unique, subjective, personal ones to tangible indexes of total organizational performance, such as bonuses paid (number per year and average amount), turnover, absenteeism, productivity, and profit. Comparisons are between the company now and the way it was and also between the company and its competitors.

Frequent and varied evaluation is essential for each member of the organization and for the organization as a whole. The evaluations provide information that serves as feedback for the people who are learning about the company and about human relations. Each bonus computation tells people in the organization that last month was either good or bad for the company. With such information coming twelve times a year, it is difficult not to begin learning more about the performance of the organization. Further, the feedback may help an individual see more clearly the relationship between his own actions and the effectiveness of the total company. Each meeting provides immediate feedback about the effects of human relations on improving operations to all participants.

Periodically and at least once each year the Scanlon Plan needs to be reviewed as completely as possible. These major evaluations should focus on what the Scanlon Plan philosophy, theory, and practices are doing for the company, not just on the number of suggestions made or the number of dollars made in bonuses. Re-emphasizing the point made in the first chapter, the company's commitment should be toward increased effectiveness, not to the particulars of the Scanlon Plan.

Strategy Principles

Along with the assumptions discussed above there are some strategy principles for initiating and maintaining the change process in organizations. These are practical "how-to-do-it" principles and come most directly from assumptions about applying the principles of participation.

In the earliest stages of starting the Scanlon Plan, two principles are: let everyone know what is being considered, and let everyone start the plan at the same time. As the company gets more experience with the plan, these two rules mean that the organization must tell new employees about the plan and permit them to participate as quickly as possible. A third major principle is that the learning-training aspect of the plan must be continually stressed, especially to management and the elected representatives on the various committees.

LET EVERYONE KNOW WHAT IS BEING CONSIDERED

When an organization is considering using the plan, everyone in the company should be aware of the considerations before any implementation is made. Obviously, somebody thinks of the plan first and not everyone can know about it simultaneously. The point is that initiating the system should be a planned change for as many people as possible in the organization. Imposing participation is likely to be a difficult task.

Each company will use its existing communication systems and frequently will augment them with a consultant to explain what is being considered and why. Where it is possible, a meeting between union and management is a first order of business for beginning any consideration of the plan. Often management can arrange a special series of meetings to inform all people in a face-to-face, question-and-answer fashion what is being considered. Frequently, a consultant can be useful for organizing, and assisting management in conducting, such meetings. The consultant is valuable to the extent that he can gain the confidence of all members of the organization and then use this trust to assist all members in expressing and adequately discussing their doubts or concerns. Before adopting the plan, as many people as possible should know that what is being considered involves risks for the organization and for people as individuals. The organization and its individual members should consider these risks worth taking.

While it is not typical, a voting procedure has been used in a few companies before starting the plan. After a series of information meetings, presentations by management, and discussions with a consultant, all employees vote by secret ballot on the question of whether to try the plan. Members of management and line workers supervise the election and count the votes. A predetermined percentage of the voters, for example, a simple majority (high risk for the organization) or two-thirds (a better risk), is required before the plan is begun.

START AT A SPECIFIC TIME

The plan involves the whole organization and should start for everyone at the same time. With everyone starting together, there are no problems of communication between those with the plan and those without.

Units and individuals are less likely to feel that others are getting a bonus at their expense. People are less likely to see themselves as guinea pigs being manipulated in an experiment. No one can point to an "elite" group in the company that is trying to sell a program. Everyone starts even.

Another advantage of starting at a specific time is that the company can focus on a specific purpose. If the plan starts at an economically "bad" time, then organizational survival may be the major purpose for installing the plan from the organization's viewpoint and individual security may be the major purpose from the individual's viewpoint. If the plan starts at an economically "good" time, then organization development and individual bonuses may be the major purposes. Then too, even lesser concerns may indicate that one time is better than another. For example, starting the plan shortly before a summer vacation shutdown would not be a good time from either an accounting or a continuity of learning point of view.

EMPHASIZE TRAINING AND LEARNING FOR EVERYONE

A major, continuing emphasis of the plan is on its usefulness as a way in which people can learn the specifics of human relations and company operations. All the situations are real, and the feedback is immediate. While trust among employees is essential, the emphasis is not on trust as a matter of faith but on trust as a matter of learning. Even if a company develops high levels of interpersonal trust among the members at one time, the learning must go on as new members are added and as members take on new jobs and responsibilities.

The plan emphasizes that individuals learn about operations and human relations continuously as part of the job experience. On-the-job training characterizes the plan well. However, the plan's emphasis on promoting the development of individuals means that off-the-job training is also important. Naturally, off-the-job training which is supported by the organization is expected to be job-related. Companies with the Scanlon Plan philosophy define jobs to include both the technical-task-related-training area and the human relations training area. Management or specialist personnel are expected to keep up with human relations research and training and to recommend applications in their organizations in the same way that engineers or accountants stay abreast of professional developments and bring new ideas to the job.

Finally, the training emphasis is on behavior change instead of attitude change. Attitudes of all the employees are recognized as important to the operations of the organization and to the human relationships within the company. However, the Participation and Equity systems are concerned with payoff for changed behavior whether attitudes change before or after behavioral change, or never do change.

Summary

The purpose of applying the Scanlon Plan is to develop a more effective organization with more effective people. One goal is to have individuals who make personally satisfying use of their present skills, abilities, and personal characteristics on the job, who improve their present capabilities, and who develop new capabilities—in short to have effective individuals. A second goal is to develop an effective organization, one which is optimally efficient, likely to survive, and able to satisfy individuals who are being effective.

The Scanlon Plan takes a positive, perhaps optimistic, view of people's potential, of people's willingness to express themselves in their work, of the benefits to the individual and to the organization to be gained by emphasizing the development of effective individuals working in an effective organization that fits them. The Scanlon Plan takes a position that development means change, and change means learning. The processes of the plan, the Participation and Equity systems, encourage efforts to reach a common goal of improved productivity. However, the new activities and behaviors are evaluated against the immediate productivity goal and also against the survival aspect of the organization and against the personal effectiveness goals of the individuals.

Several assumptions guide the use of the processes to promote learning and change.

1. Growth comes from dealing with present problems in the broadest possible context available at the time.

2. Broad participation among individuals in the organization is better than narrow participation in identifying present problems, defining the problems and their context, and in solving them.

3. Frequent evaluation and feedback to individuals and the total organization is necessary to insure that the incremental activities to make things better are actually moving the organization toward increased effectiveness.

4. The best way to bring about and sustain organization development is specifically and continuously: to work to get everyone in the organization ready to accept a program of change, starting at one specific point in time

and to emphasize the whole program as a way in which people, by being with the organization, can improve themselves—in knowledge of operations and of human relations, and in tangible financial income.

Note to Chapter 2

1. Our discussion assumes the effects are legal, moral, and ethical and recognizes that this assumption is not always valid.

CHAPTER 3

The First Condition: Identification of the Organization and of the Employees

EVEN THOUGH THE STATEMENT may seem presumptuous, the intent of the Scanlon Plan is to implement the American employees' rights to dignity, gainful employment, and the pursuit of job satisfaction within our economic system. Too long and too often the American workers have found it difficult to enter, to move within, or to influence their organizational situations. Too often work is a penalty that must be paid before employees can pursue their self-interests and satisfactions *off* the job. Any overtime is defined as a double or premium disadvantage to the employees to the exclusive advantage of the organization. Overtime is not structured as a mutual need, objective, responsibility, or ever as a challenging option. Overtime is defined as an inherently unreasonable demand for which the employer is penalized by the premium he pays the worker for the affront. Consequently, even though the employees in the United States still spend half of their daily waking life on the job, there is little opportunity for them to realize half of their satisfactions in life on the job. Consequently, the Scanlon Plan's basic conditions are established specifically to improve the possibilities that the employees: (1) can enter employment with dignity and earn their own organizational integrity and security; (2) can develop significant and inter-dependent relationships in promoting personal goals compatible with the organization's need for competitive advantage; and (3) can become innova-tive and responsible in achieving satisfactions consistent with the organiza-tion's requirements and achievements.

It is appropriate to recognize that the right to employment is not enjoyed by millions of Americans, whether they live in Appalachia or in urban cities. With those people below the poverty subsistence level, the American economy today fails to meet or sustain the right to employment.

It is also appropriate to recognize that the freedom to choose employment opportunities is not possible for millions of Americans who find themselves captive to a system. The employees can exert little influence within the system or exercise control of their employment destiny. The system often uses and exploits the employees as commodities and restricts them to their own seniority-secured job. For most employees, their seniority-secured jobs severely limit the possibility of mobility or influence on their own personal and vocational destiny. The employees find themselves unwittingly trapped by their own occupational choice and by their own union demands for employment security at the expense of influence and mobility. The experi-ence of powerlessness is not restricted to any ethnic group, such as the blacks.

It is also appropriate to recognize that the pursuit of job satisfaction is a right to pursue and not a guarantee of achievement. Consequently, this right requires not only the proper climate and conditions in the work situation but also the initiative and innovation of the employees themselves to develop and achieve this self-realization of satisfaction.

Our social and cultural values, as well as our Constitution and laws providing for the right to organize and for the assurance of civil rights, support the fundamental quality of these rights to personal dignity, gainful and equal employment opportunities, and the pursuit of job satisfaction.

The organizational psychologist is particularly interested in the imple-mentation of these rights because the implementation involves the process by which each and all employees can become effective and mature organiza-tional citizens. This psychologist would state that all behavior is directed toward becoming effective, and being effective varies from sheer physical and organizational survival to achieving degrees of self-actualization. Effec-tiveness for the individual or organization might be simply stated as the extent to which that individual or organization fulfills its objectives (survival—self-actualization) capitalizing on its means and resources without placing undue strain on any of its members. The psychologist concludes that the employees and the organization, in capitalizing on the means and resources toward effectiveness, require the implementation of these fundamental rights. Specifically, these rights are the gainful employment as the employee's opportunity for earning security, dignity as the realization of the employee's own integrity and potential on the job assignment, and the pursuit of satisfaction as the partial realization of the employee's economic, social, and ego needs on the job. Individual dignity, job security, and genuine self-fulfillment ought to be as much a part of a job as the employee's wages.

In order to implement these rights, three conditions are essential. The first condition is the identification of the work-life situation not only as a corporate objective but also specifically as a personal purpose and role. The second condition is the opportunity to pursue this work-life with the liberty and responsibility to participate meaningfully in the total job situation of the organization. The third condition is the enjoyment of belonging and being considered a significant member and, consequently, realizing the equity of his own and the cooperative efforts.

EFFECTIVENESS

Being effective is the goal of every individual in the social and economic milieu of the organization. One aspect of effectiveness is the realization of this right to employment. Historically, and for many citizens even today, the essence of life and survival is the right to pursue these conditions on the job with dignity and integrity. When these conditions are not achieved, the frustration is expressed in the demand for employee freedom—"twenty-five or thirty years and out!" A more immediate demand is for the elimination of mandatory overtime—"eight hours in any one day and forty hours in any one week is all that should be demanded. I have more important things to do with my time!"

There is frustration and challenge within the experience of every person, but there is increasing concern for the degree of frustration caused by the quality of the work-life. The size of the organization, the high rate of production output, the great degree of automation and split-second integration of the operations, the depersonalized control of processes, procedures, and communications, the computerization of production, quality, and relia-

49

bility systems without personal or helpful feedback are only a few of the work-life qualities which may seem incompatible with the personal interests, competence, concerns, and intellectual curiosity of the employees.

The low-skilled production worker, who may or may not become bored with his small, fragmented, and repetitive job, is often mentioned as an example of the "blue-collar blues." He may feel a lack of identity and involvement in, and even alienation from, the relevant purposes of the organization. But blue-collar employees, white-collar employees, and sophisticated staff members all express severe frustration in being unable to influence their job assignment, the operating system, or the establishment.

It seems desirable to reduce, if not eliminate, this incompatiability. between the individual employee's need for identification and involvment and his dehumanizing organizational assignments. If the rights of the individual employee are fundamentally sound and the organizations of employees are functionally essential in our economy, the effectiveness and efficiency of the employees, individually and collectively, require compatibility and integration, and not conflict and competition between the employees and their organization.

EFFICIENCY

We have discussed before the objective of becoming effective as a goal of both the individual and the organization. In this application, effectiveness is defined for the individual and the organization as the use or management of all of its resources without placing undue strain on its members. Achievement of what is intended is a primary criterion of being effective. The bare survival in certain economic, social, or political systems requires the ingenious application of all resources of certain minority peoples in our industrial organizations. In other systems, the progressive achievement of status, responsibility, and reward are more orderly and predictable in their use of resources, such as "keeping your nose clean and not rocking the boat." However, in all strivings toward any kind of effectiveness, the costs of achieving effectiveness must be taken into account. The least cost can be termed efficiency in the use of resources, given a specific set of wants. When the cost of effectiveness is excessive for the individual or the organization, the value of the achievement is questionable. Employees are continuously experimenting and assessing this cost, and deciding how much they are willing to pay to survive, to advance, or to achieve in the particular system. If an ambitious employee suffers a heart attack, ulcers, chronic colitis, or other debilitating illness, in his strenuous efforts to become foreman, manager, officer, or president, the cost of his achievement might be questioned. In contrast, if the concerned employee finds it necessary to coast or to slow down the production line, to peg or control quantity or quality, or to invent disruptive practices, management might be alerted to the cost that such an employee is willing to pay to gain his integrity or to maintain his own self-respect. Sometimes a strike is not too dear a cost to assure survival and some attention, or to exercise some legitimate influence over one's personal and professional destiny.

A major cost element for workers is the price of assuring self-respect and survival by exercising some degree of control or influence over one's own job destiny. The employee wants some influence over his job and its relevance to his peers, and then hopefully to his department and his company. If his influence is not real and recognized, the employee may resort to aberrant behavior to gain attention. On the other hand, he may maintain his own mental health efficiently, but perhaps at the expense of the company. The cost to the company that arises from making it too costly for employees to achieve dignity and self-fulfillment to a reasonable degree is a reminder that the Scanlon Plan mechanisms constantly bring to management. Incompatibility of organizational and individual achievement drives is destructive of bonuses; reconciliation makes it a positive-sum game.

The qualities of effectiveness and efficiency are also appropriately applied to organizations. An organization may pursue effectiveness in terms of becoming more productive, more competitive, more profitable, or specifically a leader in its industry. If, however, the company resorts to price-fixing collusion contrary to our federal laws or mismanages its human assets with excessive employment interruptions and costly turnover, the cost of achieving effectiveness is seriously questioned. An organization should be equally concerned for its sound operational health in becoming competitively effective in marketing, manufacturing, research, finance, and service, with a high degree of efficiency in using all its resources. Georgopoulos and Tannenbaum[1] feel that organizational effectiveness is based on the extent to which an organization as a social system fulfills its objectives without incapacitating its means and resources and without placing undue strain on its members.

Therefore, the clinical social psychologist is concerned with the sound organizational mental health of all the employees and the quality of their organizational work-life. The psychologist is concerned that, within an organization, the employees individually and collectively become increasingly effective and efficient. It has been our experience that an effective and efficient organization is not established by introducing effective and efficient employees per se. Rather, the organization that has a clearly defined and convincing need to be competitively effective and profitably efficient has a genuine possibility of establishing the proper conditions which will maximize the use of its resources, including the developments of its people resources. The compelling needs to be competitive, to be profitable, and to survive have been found to be convincing in focusing the attention, effort, and growth of all members of an organization toward their own individual development and self-realization and the organization's fulfillment and achievements.

The Scanlon Plan has been used in a wide range of situations to influence the blue-collar employees, the white-collar employees, the staff members, the management, and the executives, and to change the structure and quality of the work organization. The program attracts the employees' attention to their organizational situation and points out their personal opportunity and responsibility to influence their work situation. The efforts of all employees are mobilized toward cooperative performance. The organization's survival needs or developmental needs become more compatible with the psychological and economic needs of the employees. Under the Scanlon Plan, much more of the diversity and versatility of all the resources are recognized than in most situations. Conditions and communication procedures conducive to exploiting these resources are introduced.

Several assumptions regarding learning and organizational change were stated in earlier chapters as fundamental to the establishment of the Scanlon Plan. They were the growth stimulated by the needs to solve problems, broad participation, frequent evaluation and feedback, and wide readiness to accept promising changes. As these assumptions are important in establishing the Scanlon Plan, they are also important in maintaining the vitality of the Plan. Consistent with these assumptions in establishing and maintaining a Scanlon Plan, three conditions are essential for these assumptions to operate successfully in achieving employee and organizational productivity goals.

THREE CONDITIONS FOR A SCANLON PLAN

The first condition is the clear identification of the organization, primarily by the documentation of its achievements, capabilities, potentials,

52

and objectives. An essential part of this organizational identification is the conspicuous identification of every employee and his role to assure his dignity and integrity within the system. Without this first condition, the organization has no substance or reason for being, and the employees have no reason for identifying, joining, or remaining with the organization. It is also the beginning of a common identity of employees with the organization and of discovering that the employees are the organization.

The second condition is the opportunity for employees to participate and to exercise responsibility. The participation must be obvious in developing the employee individually and as an important member of a disciplined organizational team. The employee must become increasingly aware of his responsibility for himself and to his fellow employees in helping to achieve a competitive and fiscally sound organization. The condition for participation and responsibility is essential for all corporate lives if the employees are to fulfill themselves and their potential in a working society. Participation increases the likelihood of an individual's commitment to and identification with the organization.

The third condition is the assurance of equity. Unless there is a return for employees' participation and their exercise of responsibility perceived by them to be fair, the employees' organizational relationships deteriorate into armed truce, menial subjugation, or unpredictable behavior. An agreement on a formula for an equitable return on the employees' investments and commitment to the organization helps build sustained interest, reliable performance, and mutual trust.

Organization Identity

The first condition in establishing and maintaining the Scanlon Plan is the definition of the organization and its objectives. For an organization that may have a nationally recognized symbol or trademark or reputation, the defining of its identity may appear unnecessary. However, in considering the several publics of stockholders, consumers, vendors, and employees— some of short tenure and others of long tenure—identification is a process which requires continuous attention and sharpening of the focus on the current and future objectives. Furthermore, in consideration of the organization's history and its variable career events, the identification may be subject to infinite interpretations to accommodate many purposes for many people. Therefore, to sharpen the identity of the company is the first requisite to heighten and mobilize the interest, investment, involvement, and commitment of the employees and the other publics.

The clinical psychologist believes that ego strength depends on the degree of the individual's objective awareness of himself and his wholesome acceptance and actualization of himself. The self-concept depends on the process of continually assessing the total self in relationship to his environment. When an individual is ignorant of or ignores the objective facts of either himself or his environmental reality, the psychologist predicts less than adequate adjustment to the situational or organizational demands. The process of identifying or becoming aware of the organization and its history is a critical fact of operational life which should be acknowledged and confronted.

Awareness and confrontation of the facts or organizational history are not enough. *Accurate* awareness and clear identification of the *relevant* circumstances are important in defining the objectives, resources, and priorities. The various "historians" of the company—executives, comptrollers, foremen, union officers, and other employees—reveal discrepancies in their subjective perception of the history and current status of the organization.

These discrepancies must be surfaced and identified if there is to be a cooperative relationship. The discrepancies must be rigorously confronted. If honest confrontation does not occur, nothing will develop toward a productive endeavor or cooperative relationship. The process of confronting involves considerable emotional and often irrelevant rationalizations to justify past practices, entrenched positions and prejudices, and inadequate performance. The trying process of confronting is essential in reducing, if not eliminating, the discrepancies and associated irrelevant and irrational justifications. Otherwise, these discrepancies prove divisive and distracting in establishing mutuality of purpose, allocation of limited resources, priorities of programs, and commitment of all employees.

HISTORICAL IDENTITY

The review of an organization's span of experiences—durability under various demands, eras of greatness and failure, leaders and styles of leadership, its directions and momentums—reveals many evidences of its strengths and weaknesses. To have survived at all is an achievement worth noting. But what of the organization's origin and its purpose? Have these purposes changed over time by self-direction or involuntarily or both? What programs and innovations were used to implement the organization's pur-

54

poses such as products, facilities, staff, and strategies? What have been the criteria and records of performance? What are the significant factors influencing the rise, the fall, or plateau of performance? Has the work force been organized or have attempts been made to organize the employees? What were the issues that stimulated the organization efforts? Were the frustrations with the economic or physical conditions, or with psychological factors in the work situation?

This history usually gives an evaluation of management's chronological interest and performance in establishing and maintaining its reputation. Many employees are unaware of or are misinformed about their organization's history. The selectivity by management and the union in recalling the organization's history also reveals different perceptions. The history of any organization, like the family lineage, belongs uniquely to the members and gives them some realization of where the organization has been and the bases for their current status and for needed change. Confronting and working it through systematically and analytically proves to be a valuable process of becoming aware of one's self, as well as the strengths and the potentials of the organization. The identification and the reconstruction of the proven strengths and the required resources to cope with the organization's urgent need to change provide a sounder set of facts and more wholesome relationships. But, only after this candid confrontation can all the employees begin to build confidently a more functional relationship of interdependence and to expect realistically the mobilization of all the resources to meet the needs of the organization.

CURRENT IDENTITY

This historical review brings a focus to identifying what and where the organization is today. What are its current purposes and objectives? Are they realistically related to historical records of performance? Are they relevant to the current economic situation? It is common to find organizations in which management has not identified responsibly and clearly the current objectives or predicted openly the possible consequences of the current status or situation, to say nothing of programming to achieve immediate and future goals in the current environment.

One organization which has a long history for quality was found to be in this predicament. When the key executives were asked the question, "Who is your competition?" they responded after an awkward pause that they had no real competition because they were the best. When the union committee was confronted later in the day with the same question, "Who is your competition?" they too responded after an awkward pause, that they had no real competition because they were the best—a striking report of the same perception. There was no discrepancy between the executive committee's and the union committee's perception of this organizational identity. When they were asked what product consumers might purchase if they could not afford to pay the top price for their quality product, they listed several well-known companies. When the subject was pursued further and the company history indicated five years of relatively constant volume of annual sales dollars during inflationary times, it became obvious that the current sales plateau was threatening disaster. Survival was identified and documented as a genuine concern. The discrepancy between the perceived reputation of being "the best" and the loss of the customers' preference and purchase needed to be confronted and resolved. The organization chose to discount that set of facts for the time being because profits were still adequate. The management takes a dubious view or ignores the possible consequences.

In another company, a concentration of two hundred eighty highly skilled employees, engineers, and technicians had earned a national reputation for quality in the broaching industry. The employee-management relationship included a recent eighteen-week strike, followed by an additional six-week attempt by management to break the union. The employees wanted to preserve their interesting work in a most desirable community in spite of an outdated facility equipped with antiquated machinery. For example, the machines on the first floor had to be stopped to "true" up the machines on the second floor. Furthermore, the president of the organization had little interest in the situation because he had more advantageous economic commitments in other organizations in other U.S. areas and abroad.

The desperate economics of such prolonged and violent strikes and work interruptions developed an urgent motivation for job and organizational survival among the employees. Survival meant building a more competitive product, sustaining the quality reputation, and regaining all the customers who had been forced to buy from available competitors during the twenty-four-week work stoppage. It meant "losing face," developing willingness to forego jurisdictional limitations and to transfer their special skills where the needs were critical. When production and shipments were absolutely essential the union steward with nine-years' seniority volunteered to stay on his old machine that required adjusting on practically every stroke so that an eighteen-month-seniority man could work on a newly acquired secondhand machine. The young man could never have achieved the production pace of the union steward on the "old clunker" but he could achieve a good rate on the newer, more adequate machine. The employees had identified production, efficiency, quality, deliveries as the keys to survival. Together they stubbornly won back customer by customer and went on to make significant gains on their competitors, who had newer facilities, modern equipment, and market-location advantages.

Even though the relationship began with an armed-truce attitude of "I like money. You employees like money. I'll watch you and you watch me," the "old man" president eventually became more interested in and proud of this enterprise than of his other ventures. He personally escorted visitors, including his own teen-age sons, through the vibrating antiquated facility. When they had earned their way back into the lucrative auto industry, they built a model facility for a work force of nineteen hundred employees.

PROCESS OF IDENTIFICATION

The identification of the current situation usually helps define the need for change in the organization. If the employees are complacent with being the best but not competitive in the industry, they have little motivation to change. If the organization has no reputation as a stable, secure, or advantageous job opportunity and it has not identified any reason to become more attractive to either the consumer or the employee, then management can expect little change in attitude, performance, or commitment. If, however, the current facts of life identify a serious threat to survival, to loss of major markets, to turnover of valuable, experienced employees, to adequacy in tommorrow's competition, then the employees have a legitimate reason and urgency for considering seriously the need for change.

When the president of an outstanding national company came to explore the application of the Scanlon Plan, he was affronted when the question was persistently asked, "Why are you interested in the Scanlon Plan?" He immediately detailed and defended the wide acclaim of the organization for its design, products, and performance. When the consultant repeated the question, "Why are you interested in a Scanlon Plan?" the president parried with a question challenging the consultant's genuine interest in promoting the Scanlon Plan. However, upon the consultant's persistence, the president and his staff identified the genuine need for even a very reputable company

57

to effectively meet today's competitive demands and be ready for more vigorous demands tomorrow. The admission of serious current inadequacies and the painful identification of critical areas for improvement are necessary in determining the validity of change. If there is no compelling reason for change, the pursuit of the Scanlon Plan is a futile exercise.

The process of identifying what is the company and its situation today is a fundamental procedure with important psychological dimensions. The common sense qualities of the process suggest wider practice in the assessment of the reality experienced by employees in any organizational situation. A specific professional reference will illustrate the process in operation. When the clinical psychologist meets his patient, he is interested in identifying the patient's orientation and perception of the current situation. This identification helps define the degree of the patient's awareness of his reality and the predictability of an "appropriate" response and adjustment to his situation. The psychologist asks the patient, "What day is it?" and then "What date is it?" If the patient replies it is Thursday when it is really Sunday or that it is July 4 when it is really January 17 and the snow is visibly falling, the psychologist has evidence suggesting that a serious discrepancy exists between what the patient perceives his reality to be and what it genuinely is. Such discrepancies are often the causes of ineffectiveness in the patient's coping with the external realities and a major reason why the patient does not survive in a dynamic, competitive society.

This same process of asking the members of an organization or the organization itself as it were, "What day is it?", "What date is it?" and "Where are you?" are all analogously appropriate. Who is your competitor? What is your competitive status in the marketplace in price, quality, service, delivery, performance? How competitive is the organization in the job market for skilled and unskilled employees and salaried employees? And for the employee, the process would question: What is your job? How does it rank among other jobs? What is required in number of parts and quality of performance? Are you making or exceeding standard and meeting costs? What is the influence of your performance on other employees and on the final product? Where there are discrepancies between the employees' perception and the supervisor's perception of the job demands, there is the possibility of misunderstanding and inadequate performance.

Also, when there are discrepancies among the members of the organization regarding the goals or objectives of the organization there is some reason to predict possible trouble. Common areas of perceptual discrepancy between production employees and management are on the organization's profitability and ability to pay higher wages and salaries and the justification for introducing automated processes. These discrepancies tend to become exaggerated and supported by emotionally loaded encounters. Some resulting problems are misunderstanding, loss of respect, lack of trust, withdrawal of interest and involvement, avoidance of commitment, and competitive exaggeration.

The process of asking the employee, "What day is it on your job assignment and in your organization?" is the basic procedure for determining the identity of the organization as perceived by the employees. The process also provides a good predictor of the effectiveness of the employees in coping with their jobs and work situations.

If the history is not evaluated, if the present status is not accurately and objectively identified, the employees have difficulty in identifying the immediate needs and future direction of the organization or in predicting its success in becoming effective or efficient. The establishment and the successful maintenance of a Scanlon Plan demand that this process of identification be completed so that the employees can become self-critical of their own past performance and particularly of their current situation, to assess accurately the potential of the organization, to develop realistic objectives that will meet the competitive sales, operational and fiscal demands, and to organize the team that can compete successfully.

IDENTIFICATION OF UNIQUENESS

In this Scanlon Plan process of identification of what is the organization, the employees isolate the fact that in order to assure the ultimate effectiveness—survival—the organization must identify for itself a unique objective or purpose. Whether it is a service organization such as a hospital, school, governmental agency, or whether it is a manufacturing corporation of automobiles, plastic, or furniture, it should identify a unique purpose for itself. This uniqueness might be simply stated as the ability to produce the product or render the service more effectively than any other organization —that is, cheaper, faster, more efficiently than anyone else. Or the uniqueness of the organization might be expressed as the most secure, the most interesting, or the best paying job opportunity in the community. If the organization does not achieve and maintain the quality of uniqueness of product, service, or job opportunity, the publics will not regret the organization's replacement in the marketplace by the superior performance and reputation of their competition. A hospital might become noted as the best diagnostic unit, the most definitive in laboratory studies, the most efficient in its use of surgery, the most professional in nursing care. The automotive glass manufacturer might develop the ability to produce the part, which is more resistant to shattering, salt spray, and humidity, more economically than any other organization. The insistent competitive demand of the automotive industry forced one company to evaluate its history, its current mediocre status among competitors, and to decide it wanted survival in the form of job security, excellent pay, and fiscal profitability. That company has developed a unique reputation in its industry. The company and its employees have identified their objectives, specific methods of achieving them, and superior criteria of production and quality performance. There are few discrepancies in the perception of this company's unique reputation for a superior competitive product or as an unusual job opportunity. Today, the employees of this organization are producing a superior product for less money than they did twenty years ago—a *unique* performance and reputation in today's economy.

Individual Identity

In a Scanlon Plan, the process of identification extends to every person throughout the organization. The organization is its people, or the people are the organization. The organization has no personality per se. The employees direct, determine, earn, develop, become more or less effective, or more or less efficient.

In the application of a Scanlon Plan, people are not treated with consideration because it is "easier" that way. People are considered critical resources that are sought after, educated, stimulated to learn, and then held accountable. This consideration is in sharp contrast to the assumptions of McGregor's Theory X.[2] It is also in contradiction of the assumptions of permissiveness attributed generally but erroneously to participative management. After extensive industrial observations, McGregor reported that many, if not most, managers operated on the assumptions that man was inherently lazy, indolent, and will avoid work if he can. Therefore, man must be coerced by his supervisor to work, and threatened or punished if he does not work. Furthermore, the assumption is that man does not want responsibility on the job and will avoid it if it is at all possible.

However, the Scanlon Plan is based on different assumptions from those in McGregor's Theory X—namely those which are known as McGregor's Theory Y assumptions. These Theory Y assumptions are that work is a natural activity sought after as wholesomely as recreation; that men are motivated to achieve in work activities as well as in recreation; that men volunteer to perform difficult and dangerous tasks and extend themselves to assume genuinely demanding responsibilities.

The obvious contrasting fundamental between Theory X and Theory Y is the Y conviction that man's behavior is mainly the *consequence* of how he is treated; and, therefore, employees can be motivated to change under the proper conditions.

Employee behavior in organizations is more learned than inherent. Employees have the potential of changing and becoming more responsive to challenges of involvement, responsibility, and commitment. Under these assumptions, management has the primary responsibility for establishing and maintaining the *proper conditions* so that every employee is encouraged to perceive work or the work team objective as challenging as "catching fish in a cold stream," and not as punishment that must be endured in order to buy satisfactions off the job.

Once the prospective employee has identified an organization as providing the proper conditions to meet his needs for security, money, or an interesting job, the process of identification then shifts to the employee himself. When an employee reports for work on the first day, too often our cultural and educational preparation have given him no identity. He is not a spray painter, a welder, a tire mounter, a lugger. He may have a social security number. Too often the new employee is made to feel he does not make much difference where he works because he has no significant skill or experience. He thinks and feels like a nonentity. Does someone, maybe his supervisor, point out that he is a resource, relatively well paid, with considerable responsibility to perform a job to a high level of expectancy? No matter how menial the job, the company requires its performance and is willing to pay substantial money for its completion. The employee's performance or failure to perform will become conspicuous in the final product, the service, or the total effort. The loose nut may not come off during the warranty period, but the customer has the memory of an elephant, especially for a defective product.

The cryptic note rolled into the coke bottle which was finally found in the rattling right-hand door of a luxury car suggests feelings of frustration and even ingenuity in solving the employee's own needs for expression. The note read, "Now, you fat S.O.B., you can have your _____ car without a rattle!" Even though the employee-sender could never enjoy the surprise at the reception of his message, his own conjectures and stories far exceeded the real experience. Remember that the employee's behavior is more often the consequence than the cause of how he is treated.

Within a Scanlon Plan, the treatment begins with the identification of all human resources by name, by job title, and by organizational responsibility. Treatment with dignity and purpose will give greater assurance of active involvement and responsible commitment to a clearly defined program and organization.

As paradoxical as it may sound, if people resources were treated more like *machines* in some respects, we would significantly improve their effectiveness and usage. Recall the time, studious considerations, and thorough investigations that an organization devotes to the decision to purchase and introduce a new machine. The need for the machine is substantially documented; alternative machines are studied; the reputation and rated performances of the machine are obtained; the placement in the layout of the operation is studied; the security and advantage of the proper mountings are planned; the specification of the material to be fed into the machine, its tools, its coolants, and its maintenance are all predetermined; the operator will be carefully selected. This process represents intensive consideration of this new machine resource before the expenditure is even made. Treat people like machines? At least as well as machines!

Efficient management expresses particular satisfaction in its concern and accurate accounting for its physical assets. Management has seldom been as concerned in accounting for its human assets as it has in accounting for capital equipment assets in determining initial investment costs, amortization, or even accelerated write-offs. The human asset does not even appear in the balance sheet or profit and loss statement. And yet, when financial records are analyzed indirectly through wages, salaries, fringe benefits, the total cost of people far exceeds the total cost of the machines and the building structures over the twenty- or thirty-year lifetimes of the machines or building. This fact suggests the human and fiscal accounting for the people resources has been disproportionate, if not inappropriate.

Under the basic assumptions of Theory Y, the identification and utilization of all human assets among all the organization's means and resources demonstrate their real and potential economic and psychological importance and returns. In a Scanlon Plan, the objective evaluation and utilization of all assets are programmed by identifying their relative psychological as well as economic importance.

The Scanlon Plan initiates the process of making every member of the organization important and conspicuous. To most people, the president or executive officers are obvious in an organization. They are conspicuous in earnings and privilege but not understood in their functions or contributions that justify them. It has been a common experience to have people of all echelons be surprised at the critical and significant inputs and decisions required of an effective operating executive. An executive vice president was asked on the production floor just what he did? What were his responsibilities? Caught somewhat off guard, he began listing his activities beginning with Monday: "made an official call with an effective salesperson on a million dollar account; explored the required capital available for a relevant acquisition; reviewed the request for ten additional drill press machines; met with the budget committee on the projections for the next fiscal year; sat in ex officio with the Employees Committee." In surprise, he summarized: "Every day I am working to get *you* production orders, money for equipment, planning expansion to secure your jobs, money for meeting the payrolls—all the time working for *you* people!"

A humorous sequel developed when he then asked these employees if they thought he *earned* his salary. When they replied that they did not know his salary, he found himself in an awkward position, forced to declare it. Then he repeated his question. After some shuffling, they declared they did not really know, but when he became due for his next salary raise to ask them again.

These employees had become aware of the executive vice president's role and how they might identify him as a resource, a specialized resource for their personal, and the company's performance. The president or chief executive officer of any organization has a unique responsibility of continuously identifying and sharply demonstrating the larger competitive world and its insistent demands on the entire organization to perform. In this way, the executive educates the employee to his special area of responsibility and resourcefulness.

In implementing the goals and programs of the organization as identified in a Scanlon Plan, the needs for facilities, for capital expenditures, and for people resources are assessed. The staff members in research and engineering methods who could give practical assistance in cost savings are identified. Maintenance is identified as a group who could be more available to

63

assure operating speeds, full-time availability of equipment, and preventative maintenance programs to get longer machine life. The cost department is identified to give the employees prompt feedback on how well they performed on a difficult or critical job. Marketing and sales people are identified as the people who can get the orders to assure good backlogs for production and the right product mix to assure efficient scheduling and profitability. The production force is identified as the people who can assure deliveries on time, quality for promised performance, cost savings for competitive advantages.

The identification process indicates clearly the highly competitive survival game that must be won and also the "names and numbers of all the players and the specialities of the coaching staff." It points out the discipline and teamwork required to score consistently and to win the tough competitive game.

Once the organization's history is honestly reviewed and evaluated and the current situation is assessed, the question of "what day and date it is" can be more adequately answered.

A major Detroit manufacturing organization found itself in a militant stand-off position with its union membership. Eight hundred of 2,700 employees had been laid off. The heat-treating division was shut down. Employee sit-down occasions occurred daily. When the history was reviewed with management, with the union committee, and then with management and the union committee together, the employees identified how a long period of prosperity had enabled the organization to grow in size, build an outstanding new facility with excellent equipment, install complete heat-treating equipment, and meet all the union demands. It became apparent that the prosperity led to many indulgences of inefficiency, exorbitant costs, and variable quality. The clinching evidence was the identification of their unreal cost comparison with their major competitor for the Chevrolet business. It was their largest automotive customer, whom they had taken for granted too long. Now, in order to retrieve the customer's business and loyalty, in order to retrieve the jobs of over eight hundred union card-carrying members of the organization, they identified the competitive price compared to their costs and the consequent bid required to try and redeem the situation. It was a fantastic challenge! The employees knew accurately "what day it was" and what was required to assure there being a tomorrow for the organization's survival and their 2,700 members. The employees had to put the team all together again in order to earn their right to survive.

Accurate awareness of the situational reality is the first requisite to effectiveness. A research study[3] was carried out in two companies significantly contrasting in nineteen criteria of effectiveness. The findings demonstrated clearly that the members at *all* echelons of the effective organization were more knowledgeable than any and all members of the less effective organization. The members of the successful organization were more knowledgeable regarding the *objectives* of the organization and its divisions, more knowledgeable about the *programs to implement* the objectives, and more specifically knowledgeable about the *performance* of the respective divisions and total performance of the company. Knowledgeability of the total organization's reality by its members was a distinguishing characteristic of the more effective Scanlon Plan organization.

The process of identifying the reality of the organization and the relevance of every employee to this reality is a basic procedure in establishing a Scanlon Plan. However, the continual maintenance of this accurate awareness among all employees is imperative to assure the functional success of a Scanlon Plan.

Using the clinical psychology analogy again, if the psychologist succeeded in helping the patient work through his relevant history and establish a sound awareness and acceptance of the patient's current reality, that change is a genuine accomplishment. However, the psychologist knows that if the patient returns to his previous environment and fails to maintain realistic relationships, he will experience a relapse. Or, if the family or occupational situation and personnel do not successfully reveal and confront the facts of life with the patient, the patient will quickly develop distortions of the reality. The patient will resort to unwholesome[4] psychological mechanisms to reconcile his aberrant behavior to the misperceived world about him. Therefore, the Scanlon Plan procedures of vigorously and regularly checking throughout the organization to determine what day it is and what it promises for tomorrow are essential for effective and efficient survival and achievement. The continuous, accurate awareness or knowledgeability of these facts of life and the implementation of a program of confronting and meeting their demands are essential conditions to assure sound operations and behavior for the organization. Prompt and accurate feedback from the competitive situation is one common method of gaining awareness and appropriate response.

The *second requisite to effectiveness is the appropriate response to the awareness of the situational reality.* Simply illustrated, if one is very much aware of the dangerous high speed traffic on an arterial thruway but in crossing the thruway does not stop for a car with the right of way, the individual does not survive. The Scanlon Plan procedure moves from identifying the organization's current operational status to assessing the ability and willingness to change of the organization's members, to respond appropriately. The need to change must be *convincing* to every member of the organization. The need to change should *not* be seen as management's or the president's plan or program. The change should be seen as the best solution to vigorously testing, trying to cope with competitive reality throughout the organization. The Scanlon Plan should be identified as the appropriate program or tool to help the people develop an organization which can uniquely act and perform a service more effectively than any other organization. The employees should candidly explore and adapt the Scanlon Plan ideas and procedures to assure its appropriateness for their organizational reality. If this identification process is complete, then all the employees will know: (1) what the company was yesterday, what it is today, and what it must become tomorrow; (2) what are the organizational identities, roles, and responsibilities of all its employees; (3) what basic procedures should be introduced and maintained to know at all times what day it is. Then the members can co-author the program with genuine involvement and commitment to become responsible industrial citizens, with significant influence among their own integrated resources. Every employee is important. The employees are the company. Their commonality and common interest should be clearly identified and continuously experienced and reinforced.

NOTES TO CHAPTER 3

1. B. Georgopoulos and A. Tannenbaum, "A Study of Organizational Effectiveness," *American Sociological Review* (Oct. 1957), 22(5): 534–40.
2. Douglas McGregor, *The Human Side of Enterprise* (New York: McGraw-Hill Book Company, Inc., 1960).
3. David S. Silkiner, "A Method to Translate Organizational Effectiveness into Operational Data and a Test of Its Practicality," doctoral dissertation, Michigan State University, 1962.
4. Unwholesome—ineffective and inefficient—from the cultural or organizational point of view. It may be very effective and efficient from the viewpoint of the patient's attempt to ignore or avoid the demands of the environmental reality.

CHAPTER 4

The Second Condition: Opportunity to Participate and Become Responsible

SINCE THE FIRST CRITERION of effectiveness is awareness of the significant organizational reality and objectives, the process of identification is the first condition established and maintained by a Scanlon Plan to assure accurate implementation of awareness.

Since the second criterion of effectiveness is to find what looks like the most appropriate response to reality as jointly perceived, the provision of the opportunity for the employees to participate responsibly is the second condition established and maintained by a Scanlon Plan to assure the seemingly best utilization of all organizational resources in meeting the perceived reality demands.

To develop the awareness of the need for change in the organization but to inhibit initiative or action to meet the need will frustrate most rational employees. Persistent frustration of appropriate action will cause the employee to resort to defensive behavior, such as, disregard of the facts of life, reduction of interest or concern, and limited application of effort and expertise. These behaviors, though normal in frustrating circumstances, are not the best response to demanding situations that employees are capable of, and are often misinterpreted as irresponsible by management. However,

67

when an employee is prevented from initiating action or remedial work, he becomes abreactant rather than irresponsible. The beginning act of management is delegation of the task, but the act is impotent without delegation of the appropriate authority and responsibility. An employee can only be responsible when he has been given responsibility commensurate with the task. Appropriate feedback and reinforcement cultivate and direct the increasing competence and willingness to accept responsibility. Imagine what bad habits we might have developed or how slowly we might have learned to walk independently, if we had been spanked every time we fell down.

THE INDIVIDUAL AND HIS EXPERIENCE

At least two factors determine the employees' responses. The first factor pertains to the individual and his learned motivation to respond. Many employees, because of their cultural and environmental situations, have not learned that appropriate organizational responses pay off; in fact, they have learned harshly that these responses do not pay off for them. For example, in our urban communities, formal school-programs and restricted job employment have not paid off in better housing, adequate income, desirable employment opportunities, advancements, or geographic mobility. People who exhibit negative response (excessive absenteeism, school dropout, or rejection of training opportunities and promotions) to our perceived opportunities must be understood. With competent leadership and supportive guidance, these men and women must be helped to unlearn the negative response. Realistic economic and consistent psychological reinforcements of the appropriate response which pay off in meeting their needs will influence the employees' initiative and motivation toward the organization. These employees want both an economic and a psychological contract to meet their personal needs.

THE ORGANIZATIONAL SITUATION

The second factor of the response pertains to the organizational reality and its perceived value in opportunity, challenge, and reward. If there is no employment opportunity available in the community or within the organization, no program of positive motivation toward self-readiness for employment will be effective. If there is only a first-level employment opportunity available and no avenues open to pursue advancement, the organizational world becomes flat and void of challenge. If there are no psychological and economic payoffs in joining the organization and pursuing advancement within the organization, the best scientific findings predict employees' negative and aberrant response to and with the organization. In this frame of reference, the basic assumptions of McGregor's Theory Y should be recalled. Employees do not naturally avoid work but rather reach out for their part of the action under the proper conditions.

RATIONALE FOR THE SECOND CONDITION

At certain stages in his efforts toward becoming effective, the employee will aggressively seek self-fulfillment in his environment. People do discipline themselves quite voluntarily for individual pursuits and convincing achievements, such as scaling hazardous mountains, achieving superlative athletic records, or maintaining prolonged deprivation regimens. People often subordinate their personal efforts toward cooperative achievements, such as the massive efforts in the space program to the planets, peace missions, medical and communication research developments. Men and women do volunteer and initiate action beyond their own prescribed assignments—not only in the extremity of violent war situations or humanitarian crises but also in the every-day voluntary response to being needed to help, supplement, coordinate, distribute, and delegate.

On the assumption that everyone is striving to be effective, even if effectiveness means only minimal survival, employees are alert to opportunities to increase the assurance of survival or effectiveness by individual or collective effort. In this pursuit, employees would prefer some degree of control or influence over their job survival and employment destiny. The employee continually explores his reality to improve his advantage in the situation. Work in our current American culture may or may not appear as a means to improve the employee's control. However, in McGregor's terms, the work situation should have the potential of being an available means for exploring it as a facility for change and for increasing the employee's own means of control. The work situation should enable the employee to be more knowledgeable, to become more skilled, to be more influential in handling materials, equipment, and people. The employee should be able to predict consideration of ideas, suggestions, efforts, and inputs which are directed toward improved competitive productivity and profitability. This initiative and involvement of the employees does not minimize or disregard the intensive demand for cost savings, increased efficiencies, and superlative standards of quality performance. In fact, it identifies and emphasizes these demands. However, if the employees can be *helped* to perceive these external competitive demands of reality as purposeful and challenging such as the difficulty and hazard of the final ascent to the mountain peak, then the employees are capable of responding with initiative, innovation, and energy in satisfying the most demanding customer for quality at reduced prices, to keep the company profitable and maintain employment of all the personnel.

For example, in a technologically sophisticated organization a critical need occurred for increased volume of orders in the final quarter of the year. After careful consideration of the customer requirements of a major industrial customer, a proposal to manufacture a test chamber at a sharply reduced price with increased technical specifications at a record-breaking time was prepared. The penalty for failure to deliver on time was the customer's freedom to refuse to accept the chamber. Before presenting the proposal to the customer, the president called all the employees together at coffee break time and propositioned them: under these unprecedented terms, would they support the proposal? It was almost unanimous in the affirmative. It meant full employment and overtime. It required perfect timing and performance—maximum cooperation and coordination. No room or time for prima donnas. The organization completed the job two days earlier than the ninety days allowed, with the best record in quality, costs, and performance. The employees broke almost all records and proved to themselves another level of capability. Ironically, the customer replied that they had not expected the performance and asked for a sixty-day delay in shipping the test chamber.

PURPOSE OF THE SECOND CONDITION

The purpose of the second condition of the Scanlon Plan is to establish and maintain conditions that make it possible for all employees to perceive more clearly the competitive reality demands as personal challenges which they can reach and confront in their own part of the work. Participation also permits all employees to help define procedures which give them influence over their own jobs and occupational destiny. The opportunity to participate enables the employee to become interested, involved, and committed, and at the same time he is becoming responsible for himself occupationally and for his organization competitively. He is determining if there is more than reciprocal economic need linking his personal and employment goals and the organization's objectives.

PROCESS OF THE SECOND CONDITION

The process is not so much one of the organization *giving* the employees anything but rather one of *letting* the employees grow into mature organizational citizens. It is analogous to mature parents helping their children discover and know the facts of life and letting them discover themselves and their potentials in vigorous involvements and commitments in life's continuous demands. The alternatives of developing immature organizational adults, unprepared to handle inevitable competition, or of developing delinquents who continually struggle with their work society to find the boundaries of their job and organizational reality are common experiences. "To let" a child or an employee grow up is a demanding responsibility, but it is also an unforgettable adventure and satisfaction.

Influence and Its Potential

Can the employee genuinely influence his job? change it? determine it? Can the employee perform his assignment better? faster? easier? less expensively? more efficiently? Even though the employee is seldom asked, he does have ideas, opinions, and convictions about his job and organization—right or wrong. However, management generally does not expect much from employees intellectually and seldom asks employees significant questions; consequently, management is seldom disappointed because it does not expect much and consequently does not get much. Employees have been long conditioned to accommodate management.

Executives of a major automobile division have been frustrated by Mr. Ralph Nader's criticism of their products, quality, and performance. Yet, when employees on several lines were questioned regarding their response to Mr. Nader's criticisms, they expressed resentment too, but listed twenty-nine deficient items which they claimed were even more significant to safety than Mr. Nader's highly publicized items. The men on the line felt they could not influence the job or the "system." That feeling had been confirmed by repeated experience. Today most employees do not try to influence their jobs. Some employees limit their influence to supporting the collective bargaining efforts of *their* union. Whether it is economics or the strong resentment of perceived arbitrary speedup or elimination of their jobs, the employees rely on the union to exercise their adversarial influence with the organization.

In a sensitive and well-learned exploratory process a worker usually determines very early and quickly what influence he can hope to exercise in his work situation. The new employee seeks to adapt efficiently (with coaching, usually from his peers) to assure his survival in the situation.

If an employee discovers that his input and influence are accepted, he is apt to continue to explore his potential. As he initiates and continues his exploration, it is necessary that the significant people in his work situation —his supervisor, coworkers, or staff people—respond to the employee's quest with clear information about the operational facts of life. If the course or content of the exploration in improving his operation is incorrect, inadequate, or inappropriate, then the real facts of the job and hard consequences of the suggested change must be set forth constructively. Learning the facts of company life is an important part of an employee's education which requires a supervisor's time to explain, competence to justify, and guidance to encourage. The curiosity and skills of employees to pursue job and organizational problem solving are responsibilities in the hands of the supervisor. To help and to support himself, the supervisor has the resources of the older or more experienced and patient employee. With special solicitation, the supervisor can enlist the services of production or industrial engineering, production and quality control staffs, cost and accounting staffs.

If the supervisor continually uses these resources appropriately, the employees are going to be highly literate regarding their assignments and their relevance to the organization, as well as aware of the many resources available to them within the organization. In asking about his own job, the employee will almost inevitably extend questions and influence beyond himself to his coworkers and department. When these additional facts of life become identified and relevant, the employee has another dimension of interest, concern, and contribution. This dimension is not a license to go hunting in other departments, but a set of reality constraints representing, not freedom and independence, but interdependence. The employee identifies the influence of those employees in the operations preceding his own work and his influence on those employees in the subsequent operations. He becomes more relevant to his peers and to resources throughout the whole organization.

The exploration of the employee's influence has no strict limitations to his own immediate job assignments. Initially, it may seem that the engineers, the cost estimators, the marketing staff are above and beyond the industrial worker's influence. It is traditional that the engineers believe they

72

are formally trained and experienced to handle the facts of operations scientifically and objectively. When the engineer makes decisions on layouts, purchasing new equipment for manufacturing, and processing the parts, he is personally and professionally convinced and committed to the solution. He is often immune and resentful of the influence attempts of "lesser" employees. He is equally frustrated when other managment and executives question the solutions and attempt to influence them. It is true that the engineers are another important resource to the organization with great potential influence. And yet, if the influence of engineers is not perceived as available, accepted, and used, the failure of reciprocal influence can be prohibitively expensive to the organization. Too often the engineers are perceived as prima donnas and not members of the same team. The long history of strikes, of employee resentment toward engineering department's arbitrary change of material handling, equipment introduction, and standards is continuing evidence of the strong desire to have some appropriate and significant influence on the job situation. Unfortunately, the strikes do not bring the employees to an awareness or acceptance of the genuine need and appropriateness of mutual influence. Instead, the strikes develop a restriction on the spheres of employees' influence and a legalistic armed truce relationship within the organization. The parties bargain for selfish vested interests and lose sight of their commanding mutual interest in the survival and advance of the organization.

Management develops professional experts and legal expertise on how they might anticipate such employee attempts at influence in the organization. They plan programs of control to meet, offset, and compromise these influences. They consider diligently the cost of buying off this influence. Top automotive executives assembled recently to hear an international expert, who had been invited to discuss productivity bargaining. The executives ignored the expert's presentation of the employees' participative influence potential on improving productivity. They persistently pursued the governmental technicalities inherent in a legislated system. Their primary interest was to anticipate and reduce the interference of worker influence or participation to a minimum and to gain the governmental standard of increased productivity at a controlled price. Automotive management ignored the unlimited potential of employee productivity participation and concentrated on the minimum productivity gains required to satisfy governmental productivity bargaining. This procedure seemed to assure management of control of production influences at a minimum price. Management sacrificed the great positive potential of employee influence, participation, and responsibility for adversarial control in a legal contract. They would concentrate their education on the restrictions of the contract toward employee influence and the contractual reprisals for their employees' attempts to influence the system.

An example from a furniture manufacturing organization suggests the possibilities of using this potential influence in solving operational problems. The employees in the machine room had been encouraged to become more cost conscious and efficient to assure more competitive sales volume. After considerable thought and fact finding, the machine room representatives suggested to top management in the Screening Committee that, considering both cost and quality, the required operations should be performed on several small machines rather than on the one huge, expensive machine purchased by the chief engineer with the consent of the president two years earlier. There followed a lively discussion of opinion, emotion, and fact. The criteria of survival, increased efficiencies for quality, quantity, and cost, and delivery service were stated and documented to support the need for change. The influence of all members was identified, accepted, and used in the suggested resolution. Finally, the president quietly dictated the minutes to include, "to explore the possible sale of the machine in order to make available the increased floor space for production." The influence of every echelon was appropriately exercised—integrated not compromised—into a sound solution. The president also became aware of the appropriate professional influence throughout the organization. Through voluntary action to seek a buyer for the machine, the president reciprocated by exercising his appropriate influence in the organization.

The illustration points up another important aspect of influence under Theory Y. Often, management people give anecdotal or cost data to support their rejection of positive influences and criticize the irresponsibility of employees toward the organization. The steelworkers in Detroit are accused of inefficiencies, high rates of pay, featherbedding, and make-work practices. On the other hand, these steelworkers are articulate in documenting the fact that millions of tons of their specialty steel were imported from Japan and Sweden last year: that the American automotive companies have recently signed agreements with Japanese organizations to sell their cars in Japan in exchange for selling Japanese automotive products in the United States; however, all the cars to be sold in Japan would be manufactured in Australia—not in Detroit; that the United States automobile manufacturer's corporate statements were showing consistent profit improvement, primarily because of the international operations. With these facts of life, the steelworkers have indicated genuine interest and concern for influencing their jobs, their company, their industry, their survival. The company has shown some concern and put pressure on reducing the work force unilaterally. The foremen carrying out the management program are laying off men and are now known as Mr. Exterminators. Where is the leadership of the company or industry or the union in helping these thousands of men exercise their influence in becoming viable in our domestic and international economy? The employees volunteer many ideas to effect significant cost savings. The steelworkers admit the current practices which increase costs, such as stretching out the work. The employees recognize the national company has more modern facilities elsewhere, but they challenge their ability to match their productivity if given the leadership and opportunity to participate. They realize their organization is a member of a conglomerate, which might dispose of their division for tax advantages. The employees look for the leadership within the organization to help them influence their job destiny—to survive as a job opportunity and hopefully a pension opportunity in five or ten or fifteen years. They would welcome management's return to the leadership of the entire organization, to be articulate in identifying the facts of life, to establish the system that will let *every man* have an appropriate and increasing influence over his job destiny. The employees would reciprocate the influence with their participation, involvement, commitment to the total survival. These workers are aware of the candor and honesty required to define the problem but recognize that if all parties frankly admit current practices and their inappropriateness, they can together build a strong organization which can make quality decisions. Only in doing something significant together can they learn trust and confidence in each other.

MANAGEMENT'S RESPONSIBILITY FOR INFLUENCE

Management, the key executive or executives, has the greatest responsibility in identifying and making the organization aware of its own facts of life. Each executive must demonstrate this awareness and influence to the organization. Even though the chief executive may share and delegate this assignment and responsibility, he can never absolve himself of the responsibility for the organization's failure to respond adequately and appropriately to these competitive demands. The chief executive's influence must permeate the organization by alerting the employees to the competitive facts of life, and the relevance of these facts to them personally and professionally. The executive's influence can be judged by how much it releases the influence of every employee on his job, in his department, to his company, and for his industry. The organizational leader must be the educator par excellence in stimulating his members to learn and to become mature responsible organizational citizens.

EVERY MAN A MANAGER

The ultimate goal of sharing influence is the development of every employee to become a "manager." This title of manager has traditionally been used for men or women assigned or commissioned with supervisory responsibility. And yet, every employee is commissioned with supervision of his own work. To some extent, the employee "manages" his time, his energy, his usage of materials and supplies, his operations of the equipment, his production of quantity and quality, his exercise of judgment and expertise. In the most literal sense, every employee is a manager and consequently has all the rights and privileges attached to that role, as well as all the responsibilities in fulfilling its demands.

Industrial workers often resent the application of the term of manager to them, believing they are being asked to be something they are not and have not been expected or asked to be, and are being pressured to assume functions and responsibilities they are not qualified to perform. Quite to the contrary, the role of manager is completely appropriate and it is required if employees are to survive and succeed in their assignments. However, first, management must be willing to "let" each person become a manager. Then the employee must assume the initiative and demonstrate the ability and willingness to fulfill the assignment.

This notion of manager is directly related to the employee's concept of himself. If management thinks, treats, and responds to the employee and his efforts to be influential as though the employee is unworthy, inadequate, or inappropriate, management will seldom be disappointed in the employee's compliance to management's expectancy. Management directly or indirectly determines the employee's self-image. Most people respond to what they believe significant people think of them. Rarely do they take a chance and *ask directly* what the significant "others" think of them. Also, when there is a discrepancy between what a person thinks of himself and what he thinks other significant people such as a foreman think of him, the person shows a substantial lack of confidence in handling himself in these relationships. Such a person directs considerable energy, attention, and effort toward reducing the discrepancy so that he can live with himself comfortably, at least survive in the situation. After reviewing the long tradition of employees being considered labor commodities and the widely held assumptions of Theory X (workers are lazy, indolent, will avoid work if they can, avoid responsibility), a thoughtful executive will understand why employees cannot accept the title or responsibility of manager and why employees believe it unexpected and inappropriate for them to have or to exercise any significant influence on the job or in their organization. Under a Scanlon Plan, the chief executive and every member of his staff must believe in the different potentials existing in every man. The supervisor must demonstrate this confidence by delegating the task of manager with all the authority and responsibility. Then there is the possibility that every employee will become a manager of his time, effort, equipment, production and costs, directed toward the organization's objectives.

Structure for Participation

PRODUCTION COMMITTEES: COMPOSITION

As a consequence of this industrial history, a specific program has been established under the Scanlon Plan to assure the integrity of every member of the organization, as well as his opportunity and responsibility to participate. A Production Committee is established in each functional department. The committee is composed of the foreman or supervisor, who represents upper echelons of the organization and its broader scope. The foreman derives his position and authority from upper management who appointed him. The other member or members of the Production Committee are elected by the members of that department. The elected committee member derives his position and authority from the constituents who elected him. The elected representative should be the person who can best represent the department and explain its ideas for improved and increased productivity. It should not be a popularity contest. The elected committeeman should have experience, expertise, judgment, confidence, articulateness, and persuasiveness. His authority is commensurate with his competence. The committeeman's election is an indicator of his leadership or potential leadership. Membership on the Production Committee can be a special occasion for leadership development within the department and extending to the entire organization.

The function of the Production Committee is to alert the department to its own production program and to stimulate the members to produce and apply ideas for improving the productivity. The Production Committee has the responsibility for finding out the facts of life regarding volume, backlog, material, current costs for individual operations, competitive status of their operation among other departments, supply and overhead costs, machine and maintenance costs. This procedure provides a general education for the Production Committee members and, in turn, their constituents. All facts of life should be documented, studied, and analyzed. Frequent reports of the performance of the department and explanation for the improvement or failure to improve should be presented to the department members by the Production Committee. The department should be challenged to improve the current position and to continually advance. The challenge for improvement can be their own historic record or the actual quotation of their competitor's superior performance.

As the department analyzes its performance, it will discover a need for more and better information from other departments, such as scheduling, production, maintenance, marketing, engineering, and cost accounting. The staff people prove to be resources to the Production Committee and then to the department at large. Reciprocally, these staff persons learn firsthand from the Production Committee members the current and potential operating facts and problems of the respective departments. These departments prove available resources to the staff for information, costs, inventories, variances, or whatever may be needed. The spheres of employee influence can extend significantly in both directions.

In any organizational world with unrelenting pressure for production of products or service, management would be unrealistic to believe the Production Committee system would function effectively without safeguards. A familiar response to production pressure is to ignore the human resources, cancel meetings, or disregard Production Committees. Supervisors have used these tactics, especially when they misperceive the Production Committee as a threat to their authority and prerogatives.

Consequently, certain Production Committee procedures are introduced to help overcome such deficiencies and to assist in maintaining the focus on productivity. One standard procedure is to have (or to help) the employees write out their suggestions in detail, giving the rationale and improvements anticipated, dating and signing the suggestion. The writing is not mandatory. If an idea occurs to an employee during a production run, he should feel free to go to the foreman and with his approval institute the change immediately. Most suggestions require discussion, checking with others and their expertise and experience. When a suggestion is written out, the process is a discipline of thought, articulateness, and evaluation. When the suggestion is signed by the author, the signature indicates his responsibility and also provides access to the author for clarification and feedback. When the suggestion is dated, the date gives a check on the timing and expediency of the process of handling suggestions. When a carbon copy is kept, the copy is a double check on its submission, evaluation, action, and author. Foremen have been known to delay, to lose, or even to pre-empt a suggestion.

Suggestions should be evaluated frequently and as promptly as possible. The Production Committee, through and with the foreman, should use all the appropriate staff resources of the company to evaluate and resolve the suggestions. The focusing of these company resources on a particular problem has been called a work-team approach. Generally, the production employees are unfamiliar with the work and potential contribution of development, production, and industrial engineers, of the cost accounting and finance departments, of the production and maintenance departments, and of purchasing and administrative departments. In fact, production employees and many line managers are almost universally critical of these staff people for their failure to make "substantive" contributions to the program. The production employees, in their ignorance of the contribution of the staff personnel or in their frustration at being unable to get and influence this potential seriously, request the separation of the staff people from the production people as being the nonproductive personnel or "burden."

The Scanlon Plan establishes emphatically that every employee is a productive employee and that the dichotomy of direct employee and indirect employee is invalid. Consequently, the meeting and exchange of the Production Committee with the relevant staff resources is a major education in becoming acquainted with and influencing the quality and availability of their services. By solving significant problems together they have a better chance of developing confidence and trust in each other and of becoming convinced of the critical contributions each member makes to the organization's objectives. The confrontation develops an increasing sense of reciprocal team responsibility to each other professionally and personally. The work-team experience stimulates formal, and also informal, networks of communication which anticipate trouble, facilitate clever timing, and support and reinforce outstanding performance. The employees become less concerned with job jurisdictions and instead emphasize freedom and willingness to recognize and apply competence to assure the quality and speed of problem solving.

When an hourly employee begins to question the cost of the raw material —glass, wood, or metal—and recalls various grades and classifications and volume of orders, that employee is reaching for some relevant data which he does not have. His basic index is cost. What would a better grade of lumber cost (number 2 common or better) to offset the more advantageous cutting at the ripsaw or cut-off saw? What would be the cost of a piece of glass 20 × 20, as compared to 18 × 20, in carload lots if two more rearview mirrors could be cut from the larger piece advantageously? What would be the cost of a consistent SLM tannery classification of leather hides as compared to inconsistent random variances in quality which require hundreds of shoe manufacturing employees to manipulate the variances? The Production Committee needs the expertise of the cost man, the purchasing agent, the standards engineer to give them the facts of life. These staff people are solicited to check their sources, compare competitive prices for quality and quantity advantages, and to assist in the establishment and continuous improvement of material standards. The function of the Production Committee initiates the building of a disciplined work team that will respond consistently and promptly with quality decisions.

SCREENING COMMITTEE: COMPOSITION

The Screening Committee is composed of the chief executive officer of the organization, comptroller, manufacturing head, engineering head, marketing-sales head, representatives of the foremen, as well as a representative number of the elected Production Committee members from throughout the organization—production, engineering, sales-marketing, manufacturing, administrative staffs. The elected members to the Screening Committee should equal and preferably outnumber the appointed members in order to give adequate representation of the total work force and to assure psychological balance in the group.

SCREENING COMMITTEE: FUNCTIONS

The Screening Committee serves many administrative and protective purposes. In the Screening Committee, the representative resources of the company are convened for the primary purposes of identifying the operational objectives of the organization and achieving competitive performance of service and products. The president serves as the moderator to make sure the financial, facility, research, marketing, sales, manufacturing, and human resources of the organization are optimally used and effectively coordinated to achieve the goals. The president does not represent either management or the appointed Screening Committee members. He represents *all* members and their interests in the organization. The president has the unique responsibility of defining clearly the competitive status of the company from the industry and community perspective, and of stating the short- and long-term objectives for the total organization and their significance for the members of the organization.

In the Screening Committee, all suggestions made in the respective Production Committees are reviewed. Those suggestions already put into effect at the department level are acknowledged, with an appropriate editorial comment for outstanding contributions. With the production and staff resources, the Screening Committee screens those Production Committee suggestions which are beyond the jurisdiction of any one department. These suggestions would include ideas that would significantly alter the product design, the engineering specifications, the material costs, the technology, the process demands on other departments, the marketing and sales thrust, or delivery or service programs. The Screening Committee members are responsible for bringing the most accurate and critical information, data, and experience to bear on the problem. Their sources are not limited to their own committee but can be exploited from expertise inside and outside the organization. The quality of the Screening Committee meeting depends upon the conspicuous leadership of its president, as well as the contributions of the members.

The Screening Committee is another illustration of a composite work team within the organization, identifying and formulating the significant problems and bringing together the most appropriate resources in resolving the problems and implementing the solutions. The elected and appointed members of the Screening Committee should include the most knowledgeable, the most experienced, the most responsible, and the most representative members of every functioning unit of the organization. The Screening Committee should assure the objective, balanced, and disciplined effort of the entire organizational team toward increased effectiveness and efficiency. Authority within the group is best identified as competence. The Screening Committee does not absolve the president, any management head, any supervisor, or any production worker from his full and delegated responsibility on the job. The Production-Screening Committee system of the Scanlon Plan demands that each employee perform more effectively in his own capacities on his respective assignment. Every employee begins to see and feel the demands and potentials for his own improved performance. The employees sense a dependence and linkage of an increasing number of fellow employees from the top down.

The Screening Committee is not a management decision-making body. It is a fact-gathering, consulting, evaluative body that works toward problem illumination and resolution. The president is president. The president would not report to his board of directors or to his executive committee that the Screening Committee decided something. If the Screening Committee has functioned correctly, then the president is well informed, he assimilates and integrates the facts, and he makes prudent decisions which he can promote and defend with accurate and complete facts and with conviction and commitment. If the president uses his Screening Committee judiciously, he knows he has the commitment of his organization to support and to implement his decisions. He also has the assurance that his organization will use him and his office judiciously and effectively. Again by doing things together, the employees develop confidence and trust in each other, including the president.

The Screening Committee meets once a month, as early in the month as is operationally possible. A primary purpose of the meeting is to substantively review the operating facts of life. The Screening Committee requires that the accounting department prepare accurate and complete operational reports of sales and marketing, customer returns and services, costs of materials, supplies, and overhead, as well as a detailed labor bill including direct and indirect wages and salaries, fringe benefits of vacations, holidays, insurance, pensions, social security, unemployment compensation, and other related data. All these operational data are fundamental to effectively leading and operating any organization. However, figures are not sufficient. Careful and studied analyses of these data, comparison with history of previous year(s) and month(s), reconciliation with budgets, plotting and projection of trends and indicators are absolutely necessary if the Screening Committee members are going to know, understand, question, challenge, and constructively contribute to the company. The team members must know the "score." They must have the benefit of the "replays." They must recognize the "broken plays." The employee must know where and why there were outstanding, adequate, and inadequate performances. There are no hidden agendas which may produce a no-meeting meeting. There are no sacred areas of restrictive confidentiality. Personal and organizational survival are too serious a proposition to play games with. Genuine priority must be given by the chief executive, his staff, and all the representatives of the Screening Committee to the preparation and analysis of the facts of operational life and the study and resolution of the suggestions. Their actions and quality of decisions can be a major factor in assuring the organization's success.

Management almost universally underestimates the ability, comprehension, and responsibility of the people in the organization. The employees have a good degree of awareness of their situation. The employees may be misinformed, or they may make the wrong interpretation of the facts. But, they do have an opinion, right or wrong. Therefore, it is mandatory that the facts of operational life be candidly available and thoroughly and professionally evaluated so that all the members can respond appropriately, promptly, and responsibly. In return, the Screening Committee process must assure the employees that every suggestion will be received and accorded prompt and appropriate action.

Relation to Line Operation

The Scanlon Plan is not designed to be an additive or supplemental program. It is meant to permeate the operational life-line of the organization. The Scanlon Plan *per se* does not require additional accounting staff. It does accentuate the need for accurate systematic operational and accounting data, which every efficient organization needs in order to direct and manage its operations. The facts of life are found on the operating statements and profit and loss statements of every organization. The Scanlon Plan does not require a special administrator or coordinator. The Plan *is* the line and staff organization in coordinated action at all times. The suggestions, the Production Committees, and the Screening Committee are all focused on increasing effective and competitive productivity of services or products—the primary reason of justification for any organization's existence.

The Production Committee introduces no radical change in organizational operations, though it may call for radical changes in behavior. The foreman and his people should have been meeting and exchanging information, know-how, expertise, and feedback in solving production problems. If productivity is the foreman's and workers' reason for being employed, why and how do adversarial relationships develop so frequently? The Screening Committee is not a unique innovation. The *most* effective organization is one which optimally uses and integrates all its resources without placing undue strain on any resources, including the human resources. The Scanlon Plan committee meetings are natural events to bring all the resources and their managers into a periodic assessment of their objectives, performance, and projections. In most organizations, executives seldom, if ever, exercise their leadership responsibility in convening all the "managers" (employees) of the organization's resources to state emphatically the objectives, to develop plans of action, to present a feedback on the performance record, and to integrate their efforts in meeting the future. The executive officers meet regularly with the boards of directors and their executive committees. In the same spirit of responsibility, a president would seem called upon to fulfill the office of president by communicating directly to all the members at least once a year. The president may not have great charisma but he does have the responsibility to be perceived as a conspicuously good choice as their leader. Many employees look to other agencies for leadership when the leadership is so flagrantly absent in the organization's management at executive echelons. Admittedly, leadership is not an easy or simple assignment. However, like astronauts, presidents were not selected and paid for simple, uncomplicated, highly predictable and proven assignments. Executives have the great demand for innovative and creative conceptual leadership recognizable by all members of the organization. In spite of the availability of ingenious communication media and technology, most executives have defaulted in communicating their leadership role. Often they have ignored the people's need to know or they have "turned them off" rather than "turned them on" to the challenging facts.

LEADERSHIP IDENTIFICATION AND DEVELOPMENT

Consistent with the second condition of the Scanlon Plan, the opportunity to participate and to become responsible, is the concept of leadership. The potential for exercising leadership is present in every member within the organization. The situation is a codeterminant of leadership. Therefore, introducing an increasing number of potential leaders into the situations where it is appropriate—that is, within the peer group of a department, within a Production Committee of a department, within a work-team Production Committee, within the Screening Committee and its work-team

84

involvements—is a determined program for the identification, development, and recognition of functional leaders.

Regardless of whether he is an elected, an appointed, a commissioned, or even a "born" leader who has inherited the business from his father, the functional leader must fulfill the qualifications of this definition: *A leader is the person who is perceived by the followers as the best means available for getting them where they want to go at that particular time.* The definition requires that the elected committeeman, the foreman or supervisor, the engineer or accountant, the divisional manager, and even the president of the organization must be *perceived* by the followers. It is an active and not accidental role. The person must be functionally obvious, and he must assume initiative and responsibility for structuring the role clearly and obviously so there is no distortion or duplicity. He must develop a unique functional perception of his leadership.

Furthermore, the leader must be perceived as the *best means available*—three distinct qualities. The quality of *means* indicates a purpose or function, a means to be used vigorously or even "spent" to achieve a purpose. Some leaders and executives are repulsed by the idea of being used as a means by the followers. They more easily accept the idea of using other people as a means to their own ends. However, the definition is clear whether we refer to the outstanding medical diagnostician or surgeon, the brilliant scientific researcher, the effective teacher, the ingenious computer programmer, the dynamic industrial executive, or supervisor or elected committeeman, the leader is to be used—he is expendable to achieve the followers' organizational purpose.

The first characteristic of this *means* is that it be the *best* means. When followers accept a means to their end of survival, they are very shrewd and will accept only the best. When military men are on life-or-death missions, they discriminate precisely on the *best* leadership means to bring them back alive. When followers elect their leaders to handle a demanding showdown, they select the best means. Everyone serving in the capacity as leader has an exciting challenge that he always has competition in proving to be the best. The elected leader experiences this challenge more severely and frequently because he can be turned out of office when he is not perceived as the best means. The appointed industrial leaders do not have the advantage of that procedural challenge to be continuously perceived as the best means or leader. In fact, they often resent the followers overt allegiance to better leaders, such as union representatives or other competing organizations.

The second characteristic of this means is *availability*. In order for any means or leader to be useful or usable, he must be available, close at hand, tangible. If the means is remote, apparently not within reasonable dimensions of time, competence, or interest, then it is reduced or eliminated as an *available* means. The Scanlon Plan does boldly identify the elected leaders but even more conspicuously the appointed leadership of supervisors, staff members, and the executive staff, particularly the president. If these leaders do not effectively fulfill their roles of being the *best means available,* they will be rejected. If they do not demonstrate convincingly and consistently their ability and willingness to be used by the followers to achieve the corporate ends, either better leadership alternatives will be substituted or, where this is not possible, the system will deteriorate. The supreme demand for leadership throughout the organization is accentuated by the Scanlon Plan principles. The leadership may be too great a demand for most organizations.

The foremen are boldly and constantly challenged to get the work to the production people either by better scheduling of materials, parts, or setup of machines or by organizing the work into, through, and out of the department. They are evaluated on their ability to get action from other departments—purchasing, engineering, and maintenance. If they are away at meetings, preoccupied in their offices, not solving problems with the workers on the floor, the people will not look to them for help or leadership. The union leadership is especially challenged, too, under the Scanlon Plan to be more capable of representing the economic compensation and fair equity of the people in the total company perspective. Union leadership often changes when the president of the organization takes on the suggestions submitted to the Screening Committee and fields the questions regarding poor performance in any department, the objectives, and future commitments of the company: his honesty, candor, and competence are tested to determine his worthiness to be followed. If the president hedges on the issues, protects subjectively a department or staff member, fails to hold someone accountable who has been given the responsibility, or becomes emotionally defensive and withdraws or witholds confrontation, he loses his opportunity and creditability to lead.

The next requisite of the definition is the best means available *for getting them where they want to go.* From the general response of many industrial workers, their goals have become reduced to pay and retirement. The widespread application of Theory X (workers are lazy, indolent, will avoid work if they can; need to be coerced and punished; will not accept responsi-

86

bility) can predictably anticipate such limited aspirations and involvements. Leadership must accept the initial responsibility for defining the reality of the larger world, the competitive industry, the impending threatening tomorrow, and the tangible, usable reality surrounding the followers today. When these realities are identified as belonging to all members of the organization and when the means are identified in confronting and handling these realities, then the followers begin to see more alternatives in their own goals of personal and professional achievement. Leadership must necessarily start from where the people are—paycheck and security—and once these basic needs are accounted for, then other goals can be identified as compatible with the organizational effort.

For an example, the employees of a medium-sized Midwest company had little experience of either job or monetary security in their employment with the organization. Management identified with the people that their rates of pay were low in the community and the turnover rate was excessive. The employees identified where they wanted to go—toward job and income security. Leadership of the organization introduced a program to successfully compete as a supplier to the competitive, often ruthless, automotive industry. It was called SECURITY Scanlon Plan.

*S*atisfying
*E*mployment
*C*ash payments and
*U*nderstanding
*R*esult from
*I*deas and
*T*eamwork by
*Y*ou

Under this leadership program, the employees have earned a substantial and respected position in the big three automotive organizations in the U.S., as well as in England and in Europe. The employees earned the position of being among the top three paying companies in their industry and geographic area. This company usually has people on a waiting list for employment. The employees have become proficient in helping many other organizations become competitively efficient. They have significantly upgraded their education and skill levels. They have introduced and executed civic social action programs for the disadvantaged. The profits are significantly higher than average for their industry.

The final requisite of the leader definition is to get the followers where

87

they want to go *at that particular time*. Recognizing that the situation is a codeterminant of leadership and that any organization's situation is continuously changing, a leader must be alert to the changing demands placed upon him in serving the followers. This characteristic is conspicuous with the elected leaders. At the time of election, the leader appears to be the best means available for getting the followers where they want to go. Time and performance may not vindicate their decision, and the followers turn to a perceived better leadership means. Generally, followers expect increasingly improved performance from their leaders, and they reinforce the performers and reject the inadequate leaders. The employees of union-organized companies have the same demands of their elected union leadership and turn them out of office when they no longer fulfill their changing needs under a Scanlon Plan.

This demand for improved performance is not so clearly or frequently met by the appointed leadership. However, there are many illustrations of outstanding leadership by management which had been only adequate before. The Scanlon Plan puts tremendous pressure for leadership performance at every level and especially at the top executive echelon. The direction and momentum developed at the lower echelons seem to bring geometrically increasing demands for leadership in conceptual planning and integration of the entire operation. Momentarily, executives may rue the day they inaugurated this accelerated demand for competitive performance and leadership. However, the challenge, excitement and improved performance by so many people in achieving the organization's competition productivity dispel these moments of fatigue. The changing demands of the consumer, the oppressive pace of the competition, the cost-cutting required to maintain stable products, the development and introduction of technology and expertise to maintain any margin, the acceptance and introduction of the employees' insistent suggestions for improvements, the wise allocation of limited resources to the appetites of research and development—all these demands—strain the competence and capacity of leaders to be perceived by the followers as the best means available for getting them where they want to go at that particular time. Unless there is an increasing ability and skill in leadership, the organization will outgrow the competence of its current executives.

For some employees, the exercise of leadership is a slow process because experience taught them that leadership was not expected or accepted; in fact, they may have been penalized for exercising their influence. For others, leadership is a quick and spontaneous process, reinforced by every recip- rocated effort to influence his or the department's work performance. The leadership potential is in every employee. However, with the genuine heterogeneity of individual differences in U.S. work forces, considerable variability is to be expected, and the patient motivating support of a dedi- cated educator is required for the "late bloomers." The heterogeneity of America has been and is one of its greatest assets and should be encouraged in developing the leadership potential.

In order to permeate this heterogeneity of people's interests, capabilities, potentials, and motivations, communications are essential throughout the organization. The Screening Committee procedure assumes the initiative and responsibility for certain communications to the employees. The Screening Committee members assume personal responsibility for feeding back to the individual employee what disposition was made of his sugges- tion and the rationale for the decision. This feedback must be prompt, accurate, and understandable and face to face if possible. The Production Committee members have assumed this same responsibility within the re- spective departments earlier.

COMMUNICATION RESPONSIBILITY AND IMPLEMENTATION

The Screening Committee members initiate the proposal that a staff resource person communicate certain facts of life which are his special expertise. For example, the marketing or sales manager may visit the entire manufacturing organization, department by department, explaining a new company-wide product change; the cost accountant may visit each depart- ment and give them a feedback evaluation of their annual cost-savings suggestions; the distribution center manager may give a periodic statement of the inventory balance as related to current customer demand and ob- solete models; the president of the company may be requested on rare occasion to address all the employees directly to pinpoint a threatening fact of competitive life or to acknowledge how everyone's effort achieved a major breakthrough in the industry. There are no legitimate substitutions for the appropriate resource leader communicating his facts of life.

A study of the communications within a Scanlon Plan organization evaluated the number of sources, the frequency of their use, and their reliability. The communications were related to goals and objectives, action and implementation programs, and performance. It was found that the president's regular monthly letters were used and relied on significantly more than any other communication source for goals, objectives, and directions of the organization. The foremen were the principal and dependable source of information on operational programs, schedules to achieve these objectives. The monthly Scanlon Plan Screening Committee operational statement and report were significantly the most frequently used and relied on communications of performance. The study confirmed the need for discriminate communications to cover a wide range of the operational facts of life.

The Screening Committee members specifically review and edit the operational statement of the previous month and relate the facts of life to the earlier month and to the current month. They recommend areas of special concern for attention and accountability at the next meeting. The Screening Committee issues a monthly report on all the suggestions submitted to the respective Production Committees, including the name of the suggester, the suggestion, its rationale for improving productivity, and the disposition of the suggestion by the Production Committee or the Screening Committee. The minutes note specifically who is responsible for implementing and evaluating the suggestion. These Screening Committee minutes are distributed monthly to every employee of the organization to give recognition to the suggester, to stimulate prompt attention, action, and accountability. These minutes are helpful in demonstrating the heterogeneity of the people resources, their ideas, the company's resources, and quality solutions. The minutes stimulate other personnel to think of their own job, to see its relevance to other departments, to anticipate and accept the new suggested procedure, and to recognize the advantages of cooperating.

The Screening Committee members also establish other communication procedures, such as free coffee for all employees when a significant production record is broken, or when a team of maintenance people have accomplished a major equipment move or installation without the loss of production manhours, or when the purchasing agent has gained a significant price advantage, or when the sales-marketing organization has won a major account after three years of diligent pursuit. This special announcement on the coffee-vending machines of recognition of the outstanding performance communicates to the entire organization, in different divisions at every echelon, that many people are at work together. Each organization develops its own ingenious communications programs, but the Screening Committee has the primary responsibility for assuring the frequency, accuracy, promptness, and accountability of performance to the individual and to the entire organization.

Sometimes question or objection is raised regarding the time required to conduct Production Committee and Screening Committee meetings. These problem-oriented meetings are specific programs of training, education, and learning for personal and organizational development. In America, formal education is a long and expensive process, which in many ways has proved an excellent investment for the nation. In spite of our legal restrictions on age and admission qualifications and formal confinement to educational institutions, we suspect learning should be wherever and forever in one's lifetime—not least of all one's working lifetime. However, most industrial organizations have established a learning period, and even a learning curve, for the new employee. After a relatively brief period of hours for some nonskilled assignments and longer periods of months and even years for highly specialized positions as tool and die makers and comptrollers, the conclusion is made that the employee has completed his learning period. The behavior of management reinforces this arbitrary termination to explicit investment in learning for the majority of employees. The employee's interest, motivation, and opportunity to learn on the job are "turned off."

The industrial situation is analagous to the early school experience. The young child is interested in asking how, why, when, what, and who and in exploring every dimension of the school situation. By third grade, it is the teacher who is asking how, why, when, what, and who, stifling the child's spontaneous interest, motivation, and initiative to learn. Teaching is a different phenomenon from learning and can interfere with the learning process. In the application of the Scanlon Plan, the job situation would be opened up so that the worker would be stimulated to learn by asking why, how, when, what, and who. The procedure invites the employee to think rationally with the given facts of life, to be open in exploring and experimenting, to risk and fail and not be punished. Whether in an office situation or in a mechanical production or assembly situation, the reality of the job situation should stimulate the worker to ask questions:

How can I do the job better? faster? more efficiently?

Why will a change cost more or less?

What effect will a change have on production? on quantity? on quality? on machine wear?

Who could help me with a change? Who would be helped or hurt by a change?

When can a change be made? Does it make a difference when it is made?

Even though some assignments require consistency and conformity of

91

effort and do not tolerate variance or creativity, the reality of the job and organizational situation should provoke the questions how, why, what, who, and when as they relate that assignment to the respective department, division, and company.

Summary

The employee must have his *integrity* among all men. The job must have its *rationality* in the total operation. The company must have its *uniqueness* in the marketplace. Learning and achieving the integrity, rationality, and uniqueness are a continuous occupation. The Scanlon Plan philosophy and format provide one method of initiating, developing, and reinforcing learning throughout the employee's vocational career.

Every employee is *becoming* more or less aware, more or less able and skilled, more or less interested, more or less versatile, more or less educable, more or less mobile, more or less competitive in the marketplace, more or less concerned and cooperative, more or less responsible and accountable. The learning situations are not static, and man is not unresponsive. Every man is becoming. There is an ominous responsibility to allowing the manpower to become less knowledgeable, less skilled, less motivated on their jobs. Industry today is discovering it cannot afford this staggering cost of letting its employee and the organization *become* noncompetitive.

Most men want, ask, and deserve the opportunity to participate openly, rationally, significantly, in their vocational assignments and to become increasingly responsible and accountable.

How able and willing are organizations to establish the proper conditions, to cultivate and to reward realistic learning in the industrial productivity competition to survive?

Fundamental psychological problems of interest to many social scientists are raised throughout the chapter, such as, participative style of management, appropriateness and extent of influence, compatibility of personal and organizational goals, and the definition-role-execution of leadership. In the final chapters of this book, the relevant research has been systematically reviewed and reported on these issues. Chapter 7 recognizes and points out some needed research which is most promising and important in establishing assumptions underlying the psychological conditions of a Scanlon Plan.

CHAPTER 5

The Third Condition: Realization of Equity

ONCE THE ORGANIZATION and its objectives have been identified, the employees can establish their occupational and organizational identities and determine personal and professional goals compatible with organizational goals. Once the organization decides that it will let employees know the facts of life, participate meaningfully in solving operational problems, and become responsible for increasing competitive demands, only then can the employees become involved and committed to the organization and their fellow employees. Once these two major conditions are met, the employees recognize that they have made a substantial investment in the company and that they ought to realize a fair and proportionate equity in the organization.

The third condition required to establish and maintain an effective Scanlon Plan is the employees' realization of their equity, or vested interest in the organization.

INVESTMENTS: EQUITY AND RETURNS

An organization's balance sheet presents a listing and valuation of its assets, liabilities, and ownership. Assets are the property rights owned and used by the organization. The net rights (assets minus liabilities) of the owners to these assets are called equity. Equity is the vested interest or ownership value of an organization.

People who invest risk capital to begin, support, or advance an organization have an ownership value that is directly proportional to how much money they have invested. The capital investors control their equity by their purchase or sale of stock. The investment decisions are usually based on the returns on these investments and the improvement in the ownership value or equity. The value of the assets and the value per share of stock are two direct criteria as to the value of their investment.

When a more comprehensive evaluation of the investments required by an organization are considered, the respective investments of all the employees, the customers, and suppliers also represent genuine ownership values or equities in the organization. The personal and professional investments of the employees' time, energy, education, experience, earning power, and lives represent genuine risk "capital" or resources. These employees' investments are also essential and have a direct bearing on the value of assets of the organization, as well as on the market value of the stock.

The employees' investments involve more commitment of their life's assets into an organization than a strictly capital investor would advise or risk. Rather than a total commitment of their financial resources in one organization, stockholders maintain a balance among many organizations —a balanced portfolio—with freedom to buy and sell. Furthermore, these financial investors have little interest or commitment to the well-being or achievements of the organization except as it is represented by capital gains, dividend earnings, and its reputation and value on the stock exchange. By contrast, the employees of an organization generally have a limited "portfolio" of employment investments because they cannot afford diversification or even balance among their employment possibilities. The major commitment of all their assets into a single organization reduces their flexibility and control of their equities and practically eliminates the possibility of "playing the market." This predicament suggests the importance to the organization of any employee's decision to make this employment investment with their organization. Initially, the employee's investment may be limited and somewhat exploratory before the individual makes a total job commitment. The question arises as to what effort the organization makes to assure the attractiveness of its employment investment to prospective and current employees and then to assure the maximum use of the investments and the employee's returns *from* the job. The complementary question arises as to

94

what effort the employee makes to assure the attractiveness of his investments to the organization—education, experience, expertise, energy, effort
—and then to assure their maximum use and returns *on* the job. The
respective equities of the employees and the organization are quite clear.

To extend the statement of the investors, the consumers who buy and use
the service or product have an investment in the organization and anticipate
a substantial return on their investment. These consumer investors have less
commitment to the organization and often retain considerable flexibility in
changing their preferential purchase of products and services. However, the
competitive attractiveness of the purchased products and returns to the
consumers are or should be a significant concern to the organization. The
consumer's investments in the purchased products are as important as the
financial investor's capital, and their respective equities should be assured.

To indicate the extensiveness of the investment by people associated
directly or indirectly with the organization, the suppliers of raw materials,
parts, equipment, and utilities represent another important investment in
their time, energy, expertise, and reputation into this organization. When
the vendor's investment of time, attention, and effort does not pay off in
substantial volume of profitable orders, he will wisely shift his portfolio of
investments to assure better returns to other customers.

If and when an organization no longer appears to be a worthwhile investment, each of these investors can sever the relationship. If the level and
frequency of dividend returns are inadequate, the money investor can shift
his investment portfolio. If the wage and salary earnings and job opportunities are not adequate or frequent enough, the employees may change their
place of employment. The suppliers may find that they are disadvantaged
by the organization's demand for price concessions and service, and consequently they can make their selling investment to other organizations. The
consumer, who makes the ultimate investment, can be highly critical of the
price and performance of the product or service and change his "brand" or
organization loyalty for a better return on his dollar.

Consequently, an organization might be wise to acknowledge and assess
the respective investments of employees, consumers, vendors, and stockholders in their product and performance and to assure them an optimum
level and frequency of the return on their investment in this organization.
There is no reason to expect loyalty or uncritical support of any investors
to the organization.

In addition the company clearly has a genuine need for all of these investors—the stockholder, the vendors, the employees, and the consumers. There is a genuine interdependence among them, and the support and commitment of each group to the organization should prove mutually advantageous. The total resources of the organization must be administered effectively and efficiently to gain maximum returns and assure equity for all investors.

If these assumptions are valid, then it follows that every member is important, every member has a significant investment, and every member has a real and legitimate expectancy of a fair return on his investment.

Equal but Proportional Investment

The only requirement for equity in the organization is the genuine commitment to the organization of personal resources, whether they be money, talent, time, energy. Once the commitment is made in the available marketplace, then every investor is important and legitimate. The organization cannot achieve its objectives or capitalize on its total resources without the wholehearted acceptance and wise employment of all investors' contributions. Preferential treatment of any investors causes distortion or discrepancies among investors, which result in inequitable returns. For example, if the dividends are inadequate, the capital investors will withdraw their stock ownership, eliminating the capital for research, development, equipment, which disadvantages the employers. If the employees are inadequately paid, excessive turnover will cause rising costs and noncompetitive prices, which disadvantage the capital investors by reduced profits and dividend earnings.

As every employee is required to make an important investment, each also makes a *different* investment in the organization, whether it is his money, education, experience, effort, skill, knowledge, or equipment. The amount of investment can vary considerably. For example, the stockholder who invests $1,000 is quite different in his investment than the stockholder who invests $100,000 in the organization. So the employee with a college degree in engineering and ten years of highly relevant experience makes a different investment than the inexperienced general degree college graduate. Or the highly skilled tool and die maker makes a different investment than an untrained, unskilled new employee in the organization. Or the salesperson who has developed sophisticated marketing tools and a responsive clientele makes a different investment than the novice salesman going into a new territory. The organization supposedly requires all these investments

96

and their significant performance. None of these investments is superfluous or redundant—all are essential, and essentially different. Each of the investments is proportional to its contribution in the total organizational effort.

To say a person makes more or less of an investment is not to say he is more or less of a person. As we should not disenfranchise a citizen from education, working, or voting because of race, creed, color, education, or wealth, we should not disenfranchise the employees from the basic elements of job survival, participation, identification and equity because of education, native intelligence, experience, or seniority.

The system of returns on these investments should reinforce the fact that every man is important and is needed and that every man has a different and variable contribution and investment to make. The equity should be representative of the fact that as he makes a greater investment there is a greater proportionate return on his increased investment.

The realization that every man is important, every man has a different contribution to make, and every man can expect an equitable return on his investment give a central focus and commitment to the organization. The employees have identified the organization's purpose as the achievement and maintenance of competitive productivity in order to assure the continued opportunity for their employment investment and their equitable returns from the organization. This singularity of purpose to gainfully survive provides the goal which can direct, coordinate, and discipline the great diversity of investments made by many members. The insistent criterion for all employees' decisions is "what is best for the organization." This uniformity and quality of organizational decision making assures the maximum returns on the personal and professional investments.

EQUITY: A FAIR RETURN IN AMOUNT

The employees of an organization perceive equity in several dimensions. One dimension is the quality of fairness—an expectancy of *fairness in amount*. Is the amount too much? Is the amount too little? Is the amount proportionate? What are the employees' frames of reference for comparisons in answering these questions? The employees have an immediate reference to their peers, on the same job, on similarly rated jobs, or within the department. A piece-rate pay system gives a job-restricted comparison to a relatively few employees. Employees on day rates have some informal knowledge and indirect standards on which to evaluate the fairness of the returns on their investments within the entire company. Employees would

97

be advantaged by a broader, more representative, and more objective set of standards.

Recently when a foreman was complaining privately that an employee on the finishing line, Roberts, was not investing enough productive effort to assure quantity and quality output, the foreman was asked if he had confronted Roberts with his accumulated record showing a marked discrepancy with his peers' performance and the fairness in the amount of his pay returns. The foreman indicated that Roberts was difficult to talk to, was resistant to change and assistance, and felt disadvantaged and dissatisfied with his rate. The foreman was not inclined to initiate a discussion of standards with Roberts. However, after several weeks the foreman did prepare his data and did present the performance record to Roberts. Initially, Roberts was incensed at such "unfair discrimination." Disbelieving, Roberts begrudgingly agreed to gather his own production data for a period of time. After eighteen months of periodic comparisons, Roberts concluded the performance discrepancy between himself and his peers was real and that maybe he did not possess the dexterity or motivation required to maintain the necessary job performance. Roberts decided to invest in the ownership of a home-delivery milk route. Now he is getting a good return on his new investment. His initial investment in the manufacturing company had proved inadequate and inappropriate for himself and the organization. However, only when the foreman confronted Roberts with the broad departmental facts of life in fairness to the organization and identified the discrepancy in their perceptions of Roberts' performance and respective equity was he able to meet the criteria of what were fair returns for Roberts and what was best for the organization and its members.

The criterion of perceived equity of amount is also used by employees to measure and compare the investments of their supervisor, staff, and executives and the appropriateness of their returns in salaries and benefits. Some managements resent these comparisons. However, instead of being resented, this continuous process of comparing and challenging the investments and equity should prove informative and reassuring to all parties. The question is often asked "can and will the superiors accept this challenge to demonstrate their openness and rationality?" What does my foreman do to assure better productivity in the department? What do the engineers contribute besides continuous specification changes which interrupt production? What do all the staff people in the air-conditioned offices contribute? Do they produce any product or service that the consumer buys?

Standard procedure should challenge the validity of the current and recently recruited staff and their investments in the organization. If these decisions are made in the best interests of the organization, then their rationality should be readily explained and confirmed. This exchange procedure should enable these management and staff resources to be more quickly identified and used, and thereby held more accountable for their equitable investments.

EQUITY: LINE VERSUS STAFF

Discrepancies can be predicted to develop between production employees' and so-called nonproduction employees' perception of the contributions and equitable returns of the executives of the organization. Their functions, methods, timing, and locations are so different that these management differences are often interpreted as special privilege and license, and therefore resented as being inequitable. When the executive activities are documented as specific contributions to the competitive operations of the organization, that is, evaluating research and development of new products, securing additional long-term financing to meet payrolls and to balance inventories, assessing the needs for capital investments in equipment and facilities, stimulating the exploitation of current and potential markets, balancing the manufacturing capacities with the sales demands, the production employees become more appreciative of these contributions and investments, particularly as they are related to their own investments. Then the employees' proportionate amount of equity in return for their personal investments are perceived as more appropriate and fair. Where there are serious and legitimate questions of the adequacy of validity of the executives' contributions, the discrepancies should be confronted honestly, promptly, and with a minimum of defensiveness.

Historically, emphasis has been given by the production personnel to the disadvantage of so-called nonproduction or staff personnel. Currently the percentage of people gainfully employed to produce the manufactured output is far less than fifty percent. The argument is made that the innovative progressive company is increasingly investing in research, development, engineering, marketing, and finance staff. Consequently, considerable misunderstanding has developed among the production personnel as to the staff contributions and their rightful equity. Candid and detailed programs should be used to develop awareness of these relatively new staff resources and to exploit them to everyone's advantage. When a staff member asks why

Universitas
BIBLIOTHECA
Ottaviensis

the production force did not earn them a bonus last period, the degree of misunderstanding of the equity and the discrepancy in the perceptions of the objectives and operations of the Scanlon Plan demand serious attention. Under these prejudiced conditions, the production people are usually equally critical of the increasing number of technical staff employees "on their backs." Equity among all these members must be clear and rational. The relative distribution of the different investments needed by the company and the amounts of equity require continuous clarification to assure the mutual appreciation and cooperation of all members.

The equity of amount is also measured by external comparisons within the industry or community. In regard to pay, most employees do not consider the maximum pay position in the community to be especially desirable, but do find a superior ranking to be appropriate. Inferior rankings are a source of embarrassment and defensiveness. Employees are not flattered to know their organization is twenty-sixth out of forty major employers in the community or that their company is a low third in reputation among three major facilities. This open awareness of the negative status and consequent unfair community equity may be helpful in making the decision to improve the investments in order to earn substantially improved equity in amount for all members.

If the discrepancy is not adequately reconciled, there is an evaluation of the equity being unfair. Subversively reduced effort, superficial job concern, stretched time, and deficient competence on the job are only a few of the compensating responses within the organization for unfair equity. If alternative employment is available, the employee may decide to make his investments in another organization, or people looking for employment will look elsewhere.

EQUITY: EXPECTANCY IN TIME

Another quality of equity is an expectancy in time. The common experience of too little, too late, demonstrates lost opportunities to capitalize on investments. The timing of returns must be realistic and measurable for each employee. If employees are led to believe the goals will be achieved successfully in a week, a month, or a year, but no fulfillment of the expectancy is realized, irresponsible default on their equity is a reasonable interpretation or conclusion. Trust or confidence in the relationship is voided when the expectancy of equity in time, amount, or kind is not fulfilled.

Another aspect of expectancy in time is the frequency of the fair returns.

Consistent with the principles of reinforcement in learning, which require that the reward and punishment be proximate to the performance to be effective in influencing subsequent behavior, the intervals of fair returns must be significantly related to the periodic productive efforts. With the complexity or volume of current manufacturing and service operations, most employees can recall the production demands of the previous month's period, but lose the meaningful facts for periods extended longer than a month. Consequently, a thorough feedback report of performance is recommended every month.

Furthermore, well-managed organizations require systematic evaluations of monthly productivity summarized in a profit and loss statement. Inasmuch as this statement is representative of the entire organization's productive effort, the employees need specific feedback and reward derived from and consistent with this total criterion. The profit and loss criterion not only balances any internal or periodic operational displacements but also serves everyone as an external point of reference. It is important for all the members to be aware of their individual and collective responsibility in the determination of the organization's fiscal condition, which is reviewed rigorously by the industry, community, and state and federal governments. The regularity and internal consistency of the performance reports and returns can build confidence and trust, as well as sustained interest in the organization and its leadership.

The regular expectancy of the previous month's feedback also introduces the opportunity and responsibility to interpolate the findings into the current month's operations and project them into future schedules with the corrections and modifications that will achieve immediate improvements. It can provide many lessons illustrating cause-and-effect relationships, as well as establishing the operational need for management by objectives. Objectives require accurate and meaningful accountability for performance.

The Equity Formula

If equity depends primarily on the perceptions and comparisons of the investors, then there is a need for a vehicle or an instrument that can be used to put this objective of equity in perspective for all the investors. The organization is rightfully going to appear to be many things for many people. Their contributions are going to be infinitely, if not uniquely, different. The expectancies of equitable returns are also going to have considerable variance. Consequently, the instrument must be obviously representative of the life and operations of the entire organization. Its representation must be valid and reliable for all internal and external members or publics. Its form and content must be comprehensible to all people, so that the contributions and investments, as well as the equity of the members, are identifiable.

The instrument should represent objectively what all the members are investing in and doing together—development of a viable competitive organization. Inasmuch as sharing and doing things *together* is a program which builds and earns mutual trust and confidence, the instrument for representing and demonstrating this effort and its results must be understood, usable, and reliable.

Inasmuch as the organizational relationships are tenuous and usually begin with limited mutual trust, the initial form of the instrument is simple. As the employees become aware of the variety of the resources and the degree of their interdependence, the details of the instrument may become more inclusive to meet the growing needs for information. As the employees ask questions regarding these facts, as they challenge the validity of the use and cost of these resources, they are gaining essential knowledge of their jobs and company, as well as confidence and trust in the management of these resources. It is obvious that trust is impossible if the questions are disregarded or discounted and if the challenges are met with evasive, defensive, or apparently irrational answers. Before an organization can proceed to a broader-based formula, all parties must become mature and responsible in handling their own and the organizational resources and also in believing that employees are intelligent, responsible, and accountable. Employees are consistently "sold short" of the great potential of understanding the facts and contributing significantly.

Experience with Scanlon Plan applications has developed a limited number of instruments or formulas. All the formulas are derived simply and directly from the operating statements of the organization. Consequently, the Scanlon Plan formula is fundamental to and internally consistent with the entire scope of the organization and does not require special or new systems. It does require increasing accuracy, promptness, and fuller disclosure of the facts of the operational life.

SIMPLEST FORMULA

The simplest formula refers to the value of production and to the labor bill for a particular period. It represents the total productive effort of the organization and the people cost of achieving that effort. The sales figure describes the marketing-sales-customer service effort. It is qualified by the deduction of returned goods as an indicator of the deficiency in service and satisfaction of the customer. The resultant net sales is modified by the finished goods inventory which directly records the manufacturing staff's input toward the total effort.

The review of these figures at a Screening Committee meeting suggests penetrating questions. What is the marketing and sales department's program to gain and increase their share of the market? What has been the consumer response in different geographic locations? To the various products? Who is proving to be the most severe competition and on what qualities—price? service? performance? The questions pinpoint the responsibilities of the marketing and sales people and their accountability. The individual salesman, who works quite independently in his territory, responds positively to regular reports and recognition from his organization, as well as to a reminder of his expected investment and performance.

The accounting figure for the inventory variance is a refinement on the total production effort: net sales plus or minus inventory variation equals the total value of production for that period. An increased inventory adjustment figure gives credit for the production even though it was not sold during that particular period. A decreased inventory adjustment figure

TABLE 6
Simple Labor Formula

Sales —	$98,000
Returned Goods	3,000
Net Sales	$95,000
Inventory +	5,000
Production Value	$100,000
Labor Bill	
Wages	16,000
Salaries	8,000
Vacations and Holidays	1,800
Insurance	1,700
Pensions	500
Unemployment	500
F.I.C.A.	1,500
TOTAL LABOR BILL	$30,000
Ratio	

103

reports that more product was sold out of inventory than was replaced or put into inventory. The value of production figure represents the total effort of all members of the organization from the original salesman's successful effort to the satisfactory delivery of the product to the customer.

The value of the production figure suggests further questions to the Screening Committee members. Is the production more or less than last month? last year? Is the production more or less than forecast and scheduled? What is the current backlog for production? The production figure pinpoints specifically the manufacturing efficiency and contribution, as well as detailing the accountability of every manufacturing department and service area: What departments were ahead of target? behind their goal? What cost savings were introduced by engineering? purchasing? and operating employees? Is there a major bottleneck holding up production?

The value of the production figure also suggests questions regarding the product mix. Is there wide variance in the labor costs of the products? Has there been adequate accounting for product mix variance?

The value of the production figure, when compared over time, raises questions regarding the pricing of the products. Is the increase in production value due to an increase in price? Was the price increase introduced to cover material or labor costs or both or to increase profits? Or does the value of the production figure represent increased sales and production? Does the figure recognize the contribution and equity of the organization members or are these advantages consciously or unconsciously being passed on to the consumers? There may be competitive occasions when giving the customer a price concession is required. However, it is only introduced when the facts are clearly established in the best interests of the organization and the decision is openly discussed and reinforced in the Screening Committee. Unilateral changes in the pricing of the product without informing the organization of the need and effect of the change is a sure way of destroying confidence and trust.

In the simplest instrument or formula, the production is then compared to the total labor bill. The labor bill includes all the costs which are related directly or indirectly to the organization's investment in people, wages, and salaries of all members who are associated with the organization. The cost of premium for overtime worked must be calculated. The cost of holidays and vacations, insurance programs of all kinds, social security, F.I.C.A., unemployment compensation, pensions, and so forth are included. Wherever possible, labor expenses (vacations, holidays, etc.) which can be anticipated are spread equally over the entire twelve months so that no one period bears a disproportionate amount. The cost of vacations usually involves additional maintenance effort, particularly when an entire plant shutdown is scheduled for the vacation period. These additional costs should be accrued over the twelve months. This procedure should identify the people costs of doing business, many of which have been assumed to be the company's obligation or generosity and many of which have been assumed to be minimally expensive. For example, the unemployment compensation cost is often assumed to be the government's obligation, and not to be dependent on the organization's own experience from year to year. The frequent increase by the U.S. Congress of the Social Security benefits is directly and fully represented in the labor bill, including the company's matching amount.

This continuous definition of the components of the labor bill is another clear demonstration of the equities to all the members of the organization and the definition of who bears the cost of the various programs. The monthly report points out that the number of working days in any one month has a direct and full impact on the amount of production and that any loss of production time by the individual employee or the organization is difficult to make up.

A ratio is developed by dividing the total labor bill by the net production value of that period. Depending upon the labor intensity of the products or service being produced, this ratio can be higher or lower. Where the technology is well developed and process-oriented or where the material costs are very high, the labor bill ratio to the value of production will be low, as in certain automated chemical plants or in food supermarket retailing. Where personal craft skills are predominant or service is the primary product, the labor bill ratio will be high, as in custom-made furniture or in educational health-care and hospital institutions.

LARGER FORMULA

As the members of the organization become aware and sophisticated in comprehending and influencing those facts of life regarding production and their labor bill, serious consideration should be given to enlarging the instrument or formula to include materials, supplies, and miscellaneous items such as utilities. Initially, these items are generally not included because the facts have not been part of most employees' experience and there is insufficient trust and confidence in the working relation to warrant their inclusion. Historically, they have not usually been seen by management as appropriate areas of employee concern, contribution, or equity. Most employees are uninformed of their actual investment in and consequent responsibility for materials, supplies, and utilities. Management of many sophisticated organizations and small companies are not prepared and currently using these facts of life in a meaningful form to share with the employees. Furthermore, management is not yet willing to share and delegate these facts and their responsibility with their own employees. In spite of their pronouncements, management has demonstrated by their actions that they have little confidence in the ability, potential, and willingness of the employees to contribute significantly or to become responsible. Consequently, the production people have sufficient bases for reciprocating this lack of confidence and trust. Where does the equity lie in this situation and relationship?

Therefore, only when the trust and working relationships mature sufficiently, should the larger instrument be considered to include labor bill, raw materials, supplies, and miscellaneous and to develop a ratio seventy-five to ninety percent inclusive of the total production value. The exclusion of

TABLE 7
Larger or Value-Added Formula

Sales —	$98,000
Returned Goods	3,000
Net Sales	$95,000
Inventory Change +	5,000
Production Value	$100,000
Operating Expenses	
Materials	35,000
Supplies	15,000
Miscellaneous	10,000
Labor Bill	
Wages	16,000
Salaries	8,000
Vacation and Holidays	2,000
Fringe Benefits, etc.	4,000
TOTAL OPERATING EXPENSES	$90,000
Ratio 90%	

certain quite limited factors, such as profit, advertising and promotional budgets, board members fees, is rationalized for primarily personal reasons or highly competitively confidential reasons. The enlarged formula requires a vigorous and sophisticated data program which makes accurate reports promptly available. It accelerates the demand for feedback and prompt remedial action. The enlarged program opens up new and inclusive dimensions of all employees' participation, influence, responsibility, and equity.

Even though in the simpler labor bill instrument, information is also given and attention is directed toward the costs and savings opportunities in the usage of materials and supplies, no direct equity participation in these material and supply savings is available to the employees. However, the employees are fully informed on how the company needs and is highly advantaged as a successful competitor in its field when it gains these savings in materials and supplies. The employees' job security and opportunity are improved substantially by these savings and the competitive price position. The employees' total involvement and responsibility for their investments and the assurance of their proportional returns are represented obviously more adequately in the application of the larger or value-added formula. The decisions at all levels and on all matters genuinely influence their equity in the application of a larger formula.

As was detailed in the earlier discussion of identification, these data of (1) sales, returned goods, inventory variations and production value, (2) wage and salary costs, fringe benefit costs, (3) materials, supplies and miscellaneous costs are studied over recent years of the organization's history and then more specifically month by month in the last three years. This study provides an historical base which is unique and proprietary to the organization. The history can be developed as a source of the organization's identity and status. The historical status belongs to every employee of the organization and represents their legitimate basis of equity. The current history is really only the point of departure and dictates the urgency and direction of change.

As with any family or organization, one's equity suggests certain degrees of confidentiality, particularly when there is competition in securing, maintaining, and increasing the equity. Consequently, as the instruments are developed and modified, the employees discuss the importance and relevance of the facts of life among themselves. In view of the real awareness of the competitive situation, discussion also points out that irresponsible exposure and handling of the data would disadvantage, if not jeopardize, the employees' equity of job security and competitive position. Employees have proved to be innovative in protecting their own equity by discreet coding of confidential cost information and the security of monthly performance reports, etc.

Proceeding with the full explanation and exploration of the need for the Scanlon Plan throughout every echelon and every department of the organization, the employees are asked to determine whether the Scanlon Plan is an appropriate and equitable program that can be supported by all employees. If the employees decide favorably and the formula is arrived at from the historical accounting facts, then the ratio is set at the most representative position consistent with current market and production demands. The ratio position is the best judgment for the equity of all employees. The ratio is subject to continuous study and evaluation to insure the optimal equity of everyone. If the ratio jeopardizes the company's fiscal and competitive position, the deficiency in equity for all is recognized and the ratio is appropriately modified. If the ratio severely disadvantages the employee investors, the inequity is clearly defined and the appropriate change is made. However, the ratio should not be subject to continuous alteration, but should be wisely developed and documented to assure stability for the expectancy of equitable returns. Otherwise, the instrument will become suspect of having been manipulated or rigged. Such distrust will destroy the essential quality of confidence.

The ratio is not set at operational breakeven. It should be set at a level where the company is earning an adequate profit, as the company should have been earning historically. The company's fiscal soundness represents the employees' primary concern for its investment. Their personal equity is best assured by giving the fiscal soundness of the company first priority, which is represented by an adequate level of profitability.

In the use of the formula as representative of the historical position and of the current need for an improved position, what is the equity of the employees? The appropriate equity in amount is one percent bonus for every one percent improvement in productivity.

Inasmuch as every man's wages and salary were included in the labor bill, every man's fair share will be the *same percentage* of his own individual gross earnings for the production period. Every man is important and receives the *same percentage*. However, every man is *different* in his assignment and in his investment of time, talent, energy, experience, education; consequently, the actual dollar amount will be *different,* commensurate with his investment. His personal equity depends on his investment, and his personal integrity depends on the recognition of his individual differences.

It is recognized that theory is often less than perfect in application. However, the system and its formula implementation are purposely programmed to continuously encourage and stimulate the fulfillment of the theory that people will respond to work, its challenge for effort, initiative, and innovation, and that employees will become increasingly responsible.

There is unevenness of response to the program. The immediacy of response is primarily dependent on the employees' evaluation of the investment and their perceived equity among the employees. Some employees respond vigorously; others hold back to wait and see what happens. An answer to this unevenness is candidly to point out and discuss the perceived unfairness of holding back the effort. Usually, the recalcitrant employee comes around or modifies his behavior; it sometimes requires ten years. The peer pressure is a significant force.

One legal factor which may seem inequitable at the moment is the federal law requirement that the bonus must be based on gross earnings, which include overtime earnings. For the employee not eligible or required to work overtime, the bonus earnings of the employee required to work overtime is obviously a larger amount of money because that employee gets bonus on his straight time earnings *and* overtime earnings. However, overtime is a good solution for a temporary problem. Therefore, efforts should be directed toward the solution of the temporary problem and, consequently, the elimination of the overtime work and its premium.

It is also significant that every member gets the same bonus *percentage:* the president, all officers, staff, supervisors, skilled, semiskilled and unskilled production and clerical members. Each employee is sharply reminded of his membership, his personal and total responsibility to the organization as well as his equity. It is a salutary experience for every member of an organization to be reminded on a particular day of the month of his identity, his opportunity and responsibility to participate, and his equity. The extra check reinforces and stimulates good effort, modifies and corrects less than adequate effort, and sharply challenges defective or deficient effort.

Company Economic Equity

The organization's economic well-being represents another aspect of equity. In determining the formula for representing equity, the historical analysis of the company's facts of life generally indicates irregularities by

109

months, if not seasonal peaks and valleys. Too deep or prolonged valley positions are disadvantageous for all employees of the organization or its profit position. Therefore, provision should be made for the company's continuous profitable position in demonstrating that sound profitability represents the prerequisite for employee job opportunity and job security. Their equity in organizational survival has genuine priority. Consequently, every month that a bonus is earned, a percentage (15 to *25* percent) of the gross bonus is put into a Reserve Deficit Account. Seventy-five percent of the gross bonus is paid out *every* month that a bonus is earned. The Deficit Reserve is used only during a month when no bonus is earned and a deficit is experienced. The Reserve is used only to make up the payroll deficit of that period in the small formula application. The deficit months should be fewer than the bonus months; in fact, every effort is made to develop the business objectives so that a bonus is earned *every* month. At the end of the fiscal year the Reserve Deficit Account is divided among all the employees on the percentage basis as are the monthly bonuses. The Reserve is known as the year-end "jackpot." It is a kind of forced savings, which the employees appreciate for vacations, Christmas expenses, and so forth. However, under unusual circumstances when a year-end deficit exists, it is written off as a company loss, and the new year begins without any deficit, but with a revised program to prevent deficit recurrence in the new year. This method of defining and protecting the employees' equity in the company by maintaining a profitable company throughout the year is another educational opportunity to demonstrate the facts of life. It points out the unique facts of the organization and identifies where and when specific inputs are required to assure its stability and vigorous advance in achieving competitive and profitable productivity every month of the year.

Consistent with the concern for their equity in the company, when the larger formula of value added or total operating cost is used as the base, the employees divide the operating savings with the company. Inasmuch as materials, supplies, and miscellaneous expenses, as well as labor bill costs, are aggregated to represent from seventy-five to ninety percent of the total cost, a proportionate share of the effected savings is allocated to the company. Inasmuch as the labor bill is usually less than half of the operating cost, a division of more than half, such as, 60 to 40, 65 to 35, or 70 to 30 is made to the company. The exact division ratio depends on the labor intensity of the product. This larger formula and division gives credit and equity for the savings made by the employees on materials, supplies, and

110

miscellaneous, and not just the labor savings. This division for the company provides the monies for capital equipment, expansion, vigorous research and development, diversification by the company on behalf of everyone's equity. This division (60–40) is the first distribution made to assure the fiscal and operational soundness of the employees' company in which they are investing their vocational time, energy, expertise. It is an appropriate first assurance to stablize and improve their equity.

When the organization has its data and accounts prepared and when the organization is mature enough to cope with the employee investments in materials, supplies, miscellaneous expenses, and labor, there develops an even more demanding evaluation of the investments of every member and a more insistent pressure for professional performance by every employee. Executives should recognize and anticipate this tremendous challenge for substantially improved performance by everyone. They should decide if they are genuinely willing and able to assume this increased responsibility for knowing, sharing, and being held accountable for all the facts. Will the executive staff assume their increased assignment load for accountability and leadership?

The employees expect that management will handle inequities promptly, honestly, and objectively. They are aware of the pressures they exert on supervisors to correct inequities. They will be supportive of the foremen's corrective efforts. The supervisor must assure the group of his awareness of performance discrepancies among the employees. He must confront them as a group with a total performance record which is less than optimum because of inadequate performance of some members. Identities of individual employees are always protected.

In an organization that needed substantial increased productivity, this fact of inadequate productivity was revealed and discussed by a key executive with all employees in small groups of twenty employees. Because the relationship was initially volatile and immature, the groups of employees were assigned alphabetically to groups. In this procedure, the message was direct and not distorted or inhibited by entrenched subgroup loyalties or restrictive collusion. The employees responded with sharply increased production. After two years of continuous high productivity, the performance began to fall off. The primary reason was that the consistent and outstanding performers were "tired of carrying" the marginal performers. At this time a significant management person met with all the employees in groups of twenty employees—not selected *alphabetically* but by *functional* work

111

groups. Both the superior and inferior performers were confronted with their group's total production for the last two years. They recognized the accurate awareness of the diminishing production and the consequences to the company's costs and their personal bonus earnings. The group members constructively introduced their own peer pressure for performance and supported management's effective confrontation of the problem and required individual accountability for performance. The employees of the company recognized their responsibilities individually, as well as their responsibilities to help all the employees, to discipline themselves if they wanted to make the team.

An organization using the Scanlon Plan develops fully the atmosphere for the implementation of "Discipline Without Punishment."[1] It is a sophisticated concept and a demanding procedure. Mature management under these proper conditions can achieve great employee growth and response to becoming accountable for themselves. The employees learn to make their own tough decisions if they want to belong to such an organization and to discipline themselves to being a reliable team member, or if they prefer to a different set of working conditions elsewhere.

EQUITY: ONE CLASS OF CITIZENSHIP

Another quality of equity referred to earlier was the perception of fairness of the distribution or administration of equity throughout the organization. It was suggested that everyone employed by the organization was employed for a singular purpose of developing a highly competitive organization by producing the product or service cheaper, faster, more efficiently than anyone else. It was further shown how each employee had a unique opportunity and responsibility to invest his time, talent, energy, creativity, and in turn to receive a return commensurate with this investment. Often, the executives contend that they have an additional responsibility for the overall operations and profitability, and therefore have the right to an additional equity in the returns. This rationale leads directly to two classes of citizens —at least two, more often multiple classes of citizens—who fragment the purpose, dissipate the trust, and destroy the integrity of the organization. If these officers are not paid salaries commensurate with their responsibilities as documented by many authorities, then obviously the organization evidences little confidence in their ability and capacity to perform. This irregular compensation status would suggest its own conclusion and appropriate corrective action. If however, the executives have the competence and are accountable for performance every day of the working year and not just at the annual meeting, then it would seem consistent to require them to live by the same standards of all other employees. They should be accountable every day and officially once a month as indicated by the operating Scanlon Plan statement, which is consistent with the profit and loss statement. A Scanlon Plan program requires a first-class team of mature industrial citizens—no prima donnas. When production employees and line operators are expected to face up to the demands and to perform, the same degree of maturity should be appropriate for and expected of the executives and officers. The Scanlon Plan monthly returns as a common percentage of the gross savings and productivity improvement should be a direct reflection of every employee's investment and contribution toward achieving competitive productivity and a guarantee of their appropriate equity.

When multiple classes of citizens are established and encouraged in organizations by additional and special bonus systems, a system of privilege develops among employees which requires distracting maneuvering for gaining admission and maintaining executive favor. There is an accompanying intrigue of personal influence to reinforce the system. There is a strong urge to play God or benefactor roles. These behaviors are contrary and destructive to the wholesome development of a vigorous, unified, disciplined team effort or to the cultivation of gutsy dependable trust and confidence. The multiple classes of citizens and double standards for payoffs frustrate the realization of equity among all employees.

EQUITY: NO DOUBLE STANDARDS

It is difficult for production personnel to comprehend that there are more sources of returns or equity than those derived directly from improved competitive productivity. Employees understand that the "name of the game" is increased productivity and that profits are a direct derivative. They can comprehend executive salaries in excess of their own wages, but they find it difficult to understand "double takes," double standards. Greed is a subtle motivator at any echelon but seems to be particularly vicious at the executive level. Evidence suggests that the team development and performance of organizations of all sizes are advantaged when the equity is within a reasonable, comprehensible range with a single payoff for all employees.

EQUITY: GROUP VERSUS INDIVIDUAL

It seems executives become preoccupied with reinforcing their own discretionary reward system by instituting individual recognition and reward systems at lower echelons. These lower echelon employees of the organization, who have been discovering that group effort, involvement, and commitment are more reinforcing and rewarding than individual incentive rates and awards, are confused by these management attempts to single out the employees of the group. The employees find themselves disadvantaged in the group effort and deprived of their equity, which originates from their group's membership, active peer support, and recognition.

When management singles out the employee and his suggestion as being outstanding, his fellow employees often recognize their own ideas and experience given informally at coffee breaks and lunch time into that particular suggestion. They also recognize the extra effort or cooperation that will be required of them to make the suggestion work. Inasmuch as the employees see that their fellow employee has already received direct reward from management, the fellow employees feel little responsibility to second the recognition, or to support the suggestion.

In a major automotive supplier when a production employee, Harry, had exhausted the "locked" suggestion box routine with its many weeks of mysterious evaluation by a remote group of engineers, Harry decided to put his suggestion for correcting the excessive drill breakage into effect himself. He began picking up the broken drills from the department floor and in the evenings specially treating them in his basement. He produced a volume of reworked drills sufficient to supply his twenty fellow workers on the first shift. These workers had been breaking twelve to sixteen drills on each eight-hour shift and discarding them on the floor. Using Harry's reworked drills, the workers needed only three or four drills in an eight-hour shift. This change represented a sharply reduced number of machine breakdowns and machine setups and resulted in conspicuously increased production on Harry's shift. The fellow employees played Harry's secret game with enthusiasm, even to secreting the modified drills in their lock boxes. Eventually, the production record of the first shift was noticeably better than the second or third shift. Management attributed the improvement to the foreman's crack-the-whip style of leadership. Later, the relationship between Harry's suggestion and the performance improvement was recognized. Management was embarrassed by their glaring failure to recognize the facts and made an offer of over two thousand dollars to Harry for his cost-savings suggestion. When Harry was confronted on the production floor by this offer, he snapped off his machine and said somewhat belligerently, "I don't want a G— damn cent for that idea. I just want that foreman to admit we got brains and a lot of common sense!" When Harry was pushed with the question, "Do you have any more ideas?" he retorted, "Brother, I'm loaded, but that is the last suggestion they get from me."

For most organizations who have had individual piece rates and incentive systems, the employees know the continuous harassments among the employees and the exorbitant price required to attempt to maintain the system and to prevent the system's deterioration into obsolescence. The relatively few employees who can be engineered into individual piece-rate standards disadvantage the majority of employees into the "forgotten" classification. The individual system increases the incentives for secreting individual piece-rate methods and variable production, stretching out six hours of easy production into the required eight hours, sacrificing quality in the game of "getting by" or paying off the inspectors. The ultimate example of this individualized racket is the case of the widow who legally collected on a cigar box of "chits" her husband had earned but had never cashed in on his individual piece-rate system.

It sounds so free enterprising or American to put the worker in business for himself on individual piece rates or to reward the best idea or suggestions of the worker or engineer with the "Heisman Trophy Award." What is the price paid for this individual display and worker chauvinism that management encourages in developing multiple classes of citizens? Where is the equity in the system which depends on all men performing together toward one goal of productivity and yet isolates and rewards the individual?

Three illustrations best demonstrate the consequences of this programming which isolates and disadvantages the individual employee within and by his own group.

One organization had been operating a Scanlon Plan for some years when the officers decided to make awards again for the most significant suggestions. One of the most ingenious and prolific suggestors confided that he had taken the handsome trophy-prize display case home in his truck the night before until management "gets these damn fool contest ideas out of their heads again—they're tearing us all apart." In another department the same day, an unseemly suggester slyly asked if I knew who had won the big money prize for suggestions last time they had a contest. He confided that the group had chosen him as the "fall guy" and he had divided the substantial money award among his thirteen coworkers. This is one demonstration of personal ingenuity protecting their group's equity as well as integrity.

In another organization the executive officers "enjoyed" a sizable year-

115

end bonus, depending on discretionary selection of the most significant contribution. At the next echelon considerable "award" money was given to recognize outstanding achievements or contributions. A major manufacturing problem was experienced. An innovative machine might solve the problem as defined by the workers and technical engineers. After a year of hard work by a small group of engineers with significant involvement of the core workers, an ingenious compact machine was built and brought to tremendous efficiency advantage. The project engineer received the thousands of dollars award. He bought a magnificent boat but never had the courtesy to take any of the team "for a ride on his yacht!" The group isolated their project engineer. He later left the company and receded into research. The group lost its momentum and disintegrated as a team when it lost its influence and equity in their investments.

A third illustration concerned three divisional managers, all vice presidents. The organization was operating successfully under a unified Scanlon Plan. The company decentralized: with Division A being primarily volume-repetitive production, with Division B being primarily specialized, highly technical products, and with Division C being experimental and exploratory with new acquisitions. A highly lucrative bonus was established among the divisional managers. Instead of integrating the organization's great need for diversification and development of new products and encouraging the vice presidents' leadership in cooperation, support, and professional priority setting, the managers were encouraged to compete vigorously in order to receive the recognition and sizable monetary reward. Division B suffered severe market loss and employee expertise by pirating. Division C almost disappeared when two new promising acquisitions collapsed for lack of top management integration of resources and support. Finally, recognizing the catastrophic costs to the organization and to themselves personally and professionally in long-range terms, the vice presidents privately requested the elimination of the personal bonus system and the re-establishment of the single Scanlon Plan. They had jeopardized and almost lost their equity. It will require years to regain the lost ground and opportunities.

In the three illustrations, chief executives had unilaterally introduced systems which had isolated individuals and their unique investments in the organization. The system had reduced significantly the interdependence and operational spheres of influence of these individuals to their own disadvantage and the organization's jeopardy. More importantly these systems had encouraged, if not forced, the individuals to look for individualistic rewards from a relatively few people instead of the reassurance of their participation, involvement, contribution, and influence in the whole company of men. The sources, the amount, the frequency, and the fairness of their equity had been significantly reduced, if not eliminated.

Furthermore, the experiences of companies operating under the Scanlon Plan philosophy suggest that the social need satisfactions and reinforcements of belonging, group recognition, group influence are as important, if not more important, as the monetary bonus equity or returns. Two examples, one experience early under the Scanlon Plan philosophy and one much later in the experience, illustrate this finding. Shortly after the elimination of an extensive piece-rate system, and the introduction of the Scanlon Plan, the president announced plant-wide the demand by their largest customer (eighty percent of their sales) for a sharp price reduction. After a demanding question, "What do you want—blood out of a turnip?" the employee pursued the topic by asking how much reduction in price was needed. A week later the employee quietly reported a plan for effecting a major cost savings and asked a significant management person, "How much is there in it for me?" The manager explained again the Scanlon system of total company bonus with no individual payoffs. Admittedly, there were some under-the-breath remarks of resentment. However, six or seven weeks later, the suggestion was made by that employee and documented in detail how the department of *eighteen* people were willing to try new arrangements and methods to effect the substantial savings.

The employees were not sure the plan would work and they did not want anyone "watching" them. With this idea and many other suggestions, the organization earned back the entire price concession made to the customer and began earning bonuses again within six months. The group was supportive, protective, and confident of their investment and equity. Their social need satisfaction and group maturation during the six months more than compensated for the absence of bonus and matched the subsequent monetary returns. They had earned their equity.

The second illustration relates to a good volume but high-quality production operation of men and women. Under the spirit of the Scanlon Plan, the department had informally agreed that an advantageous procedure would be for all the inspectors to be qualified operators so they could appreciate the problems and sources of quality defects. For older long-time inspectors this idea represented quite a change. Some people were not sure they could "cut the mustard" on production. However, they did meet and beat the

117

standard with considerable "free" instruction. The entire department soon was not only making standards in quantity and quality but exceeding them consistently from fifteen to eighteen percent—a great accomplishment! The employees "got to their foreman," an excellent supervisor, and informed him not to interfere—more importantly, they instructed him "don't let top management or personnel interfere or increase our pay rates in merit rating; we are a team and we will take our earnings out in Scanlon bonuses. If someone moves in on us, we will drop back to zero or standard and peg it right on the nose. If you need more production, let us know—we are going to stick in there!"

The employees' rhythm, pace, and expertise are conspicuous even to an untrained observer. Their investments of effort, time, and experience are being made significantly, and they exercise considerable control, discipline, and influence. The employees recognize their equity in the well-being of their own group and the organization at large. The group response and their company influence are especially meaningful to them.

There are indications that the shift from the entrepreneurial independence of the pieceworker to the social interdependence of the Scanlon organization man is not without the worker's misgivings. After several years of operating under the Scanlon Plan, a highly skilled former pieceworker confided he was not always sure of his preference for the group program. He explained that under the piece-rate system, if you had a lousy production day, no one else was hurt and if you had a good day that was money in "your own bank." Now, under the Scanlon Plan if you have a lousy production day, you "reckon that night that you let down a lot of other people and maybe it disturbs you." When asked if he would prefer to return to piece rates, he quickly and smiling replied, "H—, No! Why even on my poorest day now I beat my best piece-rate day. It really keeps us all pulling together. I'm not losing any sleep."

Again, there are not *two* classes of citizens, the employees on piece rates versus the employees on day rates, or the direct workers versus indirect workers, or the production workers versus nonproduction workers, the line workers versus the staff workers, the workers versus management, us versus them. The investment of every employee in the organization and his assurance of everyone's equity in amount, frequency, and kind become increasingly his own best interest.

NEGATIVE EQUITY

Returns or equity can be negative. All does not always go well. If the performance of any group is significantly inadequate or the total company's effort does not compete successfully, then the returns are negative. The feedback of critical information and specific performance failures are clearly negative returns. The important aspect is the group's confident feeling of ability and willingness to alter the negative situation. Often, and maybe more often, negative returns stimulate greater breakthroughs and achievements than continuous records of success. Experience shows that when an organization is tackling a new product breakthrough, major model change, a challenging order for the most demanding customer or salvaging an obsolete operation, there are periods of reduced or no monetary returns. Under the proper guidance, these conditions can attract more employee investment of interest, expertise, effort, and competence and can produce tremendous personal and professional returns for the employees in again getting on top of the problem and the competition. Their investments and returns are threatened. The employees will act to protect their equity.

WAGES: MANAGEMENT PREROGATIVE OR PERSONAL EQUITY RESPONSIBILITY

There is another distinction of equity which is directly promoted by the application of the Scanlon Plan and its formula. There is a long-standing myth that management or organization ownership are the guardians of the company's largess and the purveyors of wage and salary increases. It is often perceived and handled as though it were the prerogative, if not the responsibility, of management in its unique wisdom to distribute these monetary rewards, or to withhold them. The common terminology in collective bargaining is "what is the company going to *give* and what can the union get out of management."

Once the facts of operational life in the Scanlon Plan are made available and understandable, it becomes quite clear to employees that management has no special powers or legitimate claim in the exercise of this dispensation or money distribution. In fact, it is incumbent upon *all* employees of the organization to develop and earn the capacity of the company to pay current or increased wages and salaries. If the company is not in a competitive position to secure and maintain its markets, it has no resources to meet the payroll. If the employee investors do not put money in the bank (increased productivity, cost savings, and profits by their efforts), they cannot "write checks on their own account." The employees specifically control their equity.

How many companies objectively and overtly talk and plan wage and salary increases a year in advance of the increased wage package becoming due or expected? It is a reasonable procedure for so sizable and important an expenditure in any organization's budget. If the monies must be earned before they are disbursed, a year is not too long a time to earn or accumulate them. Once the approximate amount is determined as related to the competitive realities of the industry and community, then it is appropriate to work through every echelon and every department the actual cost savings they individually and collectively can achieve on materials, supplies, miscellaneous, and labor. It is not a case of department heads manipulating the figures with their pencils, guesstimating percentages. It means beginning at the top executives and through the lowest echelons using dollars and cents to work through specific ideas and suggestions on the actual operations. If the wage package is over a million dollars for the corporation, what is each division's and each department's proportionate share in the required cost savings? $127,000? $52,000? These savings suggestions should be submitted a year in advance of the payoff package date. Then the cost accounting department works with each department extending, more often shrinking, the anticipated savings that can be realistically expected in view of sales forecasts, seasonal demands, burden commitments, and other contingencies. The Scanlon facts-of-life monthly reports should specifically detail the progress toward these cost savings estimates of the respective departments and divisions toward the organization's total cost savings objective for the wage package.

In this procedure, the exact investment of time, energy, effort, expertise, and suggestions of every employee is carefully documented in order to assure realistically the equity in amount on an expected date, and in fairness relative to the entire organization. For such well-managed organizations, there are no "surprises" which then destroy the trust and confidence in the individual and corporate equity. There are no Santa Claus gifts or autocratic benefactor's bonuses. There are disciplined team members who are being intelligently coached to win the game. The employees know what the plays are, how to execute them, and how to score. The employees know the score at all times, whether they are ahead or behind the competition.

There is a supplementary experience under a Scanlon Plan which occurs with some frequency in the administration of standards. Contrary to some understandings, standards are not inconsistent with a Scanlon Plan if they are used as a tool for meeting the cost and not for restrictive control. Everyone needs a benchmark and a set of criteria to evaluate himself and his organization—to know accurately "what day it is" in his organizational world. Without realistic and continuous reference to the outside world, it is easy to lose perspective and objective orientation. Standards should be used *with* people to achieve a mutually advantageous purpose, thereby helping the employees to gain awareness and confidence in themselves and with others.

Industrial engineers complain bitterly, "Why don't those employees trust me out there on the production floor? Don't they know I'm trying to help them?" As long as industrial engineers put standards *on* employees instead of *with* employees, they will be mistrusted. How often does an industrial engineer admit the subjectivity and fallibility of his standard? What is even more important, how often do industrial engineers admit and show that the validity of their standards is directly related to the competitive cost required by the customer?

A standard has a primary validity in being related to what is the competitive cost. Too often engineers consider standards to be their scientific province and an end rather than a means toward achieving a competitive-cost end. Standards involve subjective judgments and, therefore, ought to be shared with the performer as he experiences it as well as the scientific engineer as he observes it. If the standard does not belong to the performer, the standard has little utility or potential for the organization. A standard should be established to be met not as the ultimate of engineering expertise, but to be exceeded for the cost advantage to everyone.

Often, the engineering department in administering standards or measured day-work programs enthusiastically claims that, based on *their* standards, the individual employee's earnings are limited only by his own effort, Also, the company can continuously afford to pay him more if the employee exceeds his standard. Two cautions are suggested in helping the employee comprehend the whole competitive reality: (1) the standards be continually validated with competitive costs, and (2) the competitive position and profitability of the entire operation be determined and confronted. If the departments on standard are out of phase because of excessive material or

121

supply usage, because of inadequate quality and excessive rejects, or unabsorbed burden—and the total operation is not competitive and is unprofitable—then the standards are a hoax. The workers may be exceeding standards with abandon and with the apparent assurance that over 125 percent is good for everyone. They may be killing the goose that laid the golden egg in their excessive material costs, burden, and so forth. This procedure is absolute deceit in not giving the employees all the facts of life and inferring assurance of their own security being dependent exclusively on their efforts and performance related to an isolated subjective standard. It is not surprising that employees cannot comprehend abrupt layoffs or discontinuance of operations because the company is losing money when "I'm beating my standard." Any discrepancy between the total profitability and efficiency of the operations and the employees' earnings must be reconciled. The failure to reconcile and integrate these facts is a fraudulent disregard and destruction of equity, as well as of organizational confidence and trust.

EQUITY: MISCELLANEOUS CONSIDERATIONS

Two general questions often arise regarding equity during the analysis and application of the Scanlon formula. The first question asks why should the executives who are obviously very adequately paid be included in the Scanlon Plan bonus to receive even more money? Is it equitable, by applying a percentage on their larger base, for them consequently to receive a larger money amount than anyone else? The arithmetic answer to the equity is that the executives take out of the bonus pool only in proportion to what their respective salaries put into the participating payroll.

For example, if the monthly payroll is $100,000 including every employee and the president and it is $96,000 including every employee except the president, the ratio against a $400,000 sales value of production would be twenty-five percent in the case with the president and twenty-four percent in the case without the president. Applying the respective ratios to a monthly sales value of production of $500,000, the allowed labor in the case with the president would be $125,000 and in the case without the president would be $120,000. The actual payroll charge against these allowances would be $100,000 and $96,000, providing bonus pools for distribution of $25,000 and $24,000 respectively. The respective bonus pools divided by the allowed payrolls of $100,000 and $96,000 result in the same *percentage—twenty-five percent*. Consequently, all participating employees realize the *same percentage* on their own individual gross earnings—twenty-five percent—whether the president's salary is included or excluded. Each employee would receive the same proportionate amount in his special bonus check.

However, arithmetic or economic equity is only a limited representation. The psychological equity of the president or executive being a significant member of the team and accountable for a major contribution must be represented. The executive, being human and also responsive to social motivations of belonging, recognition, involvement, and commitment, needs to realize specifically his required investments of expertise, competence, and leadership and then his proportionate equity. The employees need to have access to the chief executive, to influence him, as well as be influenced responsibly by him. When the monthly Scanlon statement is made, the chief executive knows whether the entire team effort has been productive. If it is positive equity, the president as well as every man in the organization is reinforced in his job efforts; if it is negative equity, the president is stimulated to work more diligently with the team to correct the situation. It is clear that everyone is needed, and there must be equity for everyone to assure the sustained investment and accountability of everyone.

The second question is why not divide the bonus returns equally in amount to everyone. The idea has an initial appeal of parsimonious fairness. However, this procedure would be in contradiction to the basic fact that everyone is different, and that everyone has a different ability and willingness to invest his talent, education, skill, knowledge, competence, experience, and judgment into the organization. Simply illustrated, as the very skilled employee with twenty years of specialized tool and die training and experience has more ability and responsibility to contribute than a young, inexperienced, unskilled new employee, it is only fair to recognize the difference in deserved and expected equity.

The percentage of the bonus is the same for every employee, but the actual amount of bonus is proportional to the ability and willingness to invest in the organization.

Individuals in the family, in school, and especially in the work situation want recognition of their identity and integrity. The team of employees and the organization are more wholesomely realistic and professionally advantaged by the recognition and reinforcement of the heterogeneity of people resources required. Sound job evaluation procedures implement this concept of differential human performance and proportionate equity.

Furthermore, federal wage and hour laws stipulate specifically that such bonus returns shall be paid on *gross* earnings.

Summary

In summary, equity is the capstone to the three psychological conditions required to establish and maintain a Scanlon Plan. The first condition, the identification of an organization and its objectives, is unproductive unless the employees are given the opportunity to participate and become responsible. The second condition, the opportunity to participate and become responsible, loses validity and vitality without the third condition—that employees realize a meaningful and regular equity in the organization.

All three conditions are essential to the successful operation of a Scanlon Plan. The sequence of the introduction of the three conditions is logically directed toward the individual and organizational developments. The sequence is not absolute or mutually exclusive for each condition. On the contrary, the three conditions of identification, provision of the opportunity to participate, and earning an equity are continuously ongoing and changing in emphasis in response to the demands for organizational change. The three conditions facilitate and expedite the process of change required for today's reality of competition and for tomorrow's predictable accelerated challenges.

The conditions operating in a Scanlon Plan have demonstrated the possibilities of assuring the important right to a more secure and significant employment opportunity. These job opportunities enable the employees to exercise increasing influence and responsibility. The right is further assured in the employees' purposeful identity as significant first-class members of the organization.

The right to become a responsible organizational citizen is developed by providing on-the-job opportunities to participate in making significant contributions in ideas, suggestions, efforts, time, expertise. This right is increasingly extended on the job and in the organization as the employees develop and demonstrate competence and responsibility in fulfilling assignments.

The right to pursue satisfaction on the job is an exciting and endless opportunity to confront and vie with realistic competition. Inasmuch as competition and the consequent demand for change are endless, the guarantee is for the pursuit and not for the achievement of satisfaction on the job.

The relevance of equity to the human behavior in any setting is a subject of wide interest. The topic of incentives has been closely associated with considerations of equity. The characteristics of equity and incentives as

represented by time, amount, and administration, expectancies and fulfillment are the concerns of the theoretical researchers and organizational
administrators. The equity research related to the Scanlon Plan has been
minimal to date as is reported in the following chapter. The research
possibilities are only implied and have not been exploited so far. The final
chapter is aimed toward stimulating research on this subject of equity in any
organizational setting.

The Scanlon Plan, consistent with Theory Y's assumptions, is a highly
demanding philosophy of management. Contrary to being permissive, it is
insistent on superior performance toward the organization's objectives.
It is critical of the adequacy and utilization of all of its resources. It is in-
tolerant of incompetence and particularly familial nepotism. It requires
aggressive participation, involvement, and commitment in being sharply
accountable. It encourages, cultivates, and rewards psychologically and
economically individual and collective discipline and responsibility. It develops the continual awareness of and the capacity for change throughout
the organization.

NOTE TO CHAPTER 5

1.   John Huberman, "Discipline Without Punishment," *Harvard Business Review* (July-
      Aug. 1964), 42(4): 62–68.

CHAPTER 6

Previous Research on the Scanlon Plan

IN PREVIOUS CHAPTERS the theory and application of the Scanlon Plan have been discussed in detail. The potential contributions of the Scanlon Plan to organizational effectiveness and individual performance and satisfaction, as well as the problems frequently encountered in attempting to implement the plan, have received a good deal of attention. However, this attention has been based on the rational analysis of the authors' practical experiences with organizations and their general knowledge of social science theory and research. Little attention has been specifically devoted to the discussion of research related to the Scanlon Plan. If we were exclusively advocates of the Scanlon Plan, we would very likely have little interest in such a discussion. However, we are not exclusively advocates. We are also social scientists, who are committed to increasing knowledge about organizations and people in general and about the Scanlon Plan in particular through objective, scientific research. This commitment is not primarily based on belief in the intrinsic merits of scientific research, although we do hold such beliefs. Certainly we would not suggest, at least not with any expectation of having the suggestion taken seriously, that professional managers should be actively interested in scientific research because of its intrinsic merits. Rather, our commitment to scientific research on the Scan-

126

lon Plan and our reason for urging managers to be interested in such research is based on the conviction that such research is essential for improved application. That is, objective, scientific research is necessary for significant progress in the development of social and organizational "technology," just as it is for progress in physical technology. The spectacular achievements of our space program would obviously not have been possible without the substantial progress in physical science knowledge which preceded it. Similarly, we cannot count on long-run progress in human and organizational affairs, including the implementation of the Scanlon Plan, without increased social science knowledge.

The purpose of this chapter, therefore, is to review the previous research related to the Scanlon Plan and to discuss the most fruitful directions for future research in this area. The relevant research literature is diverse. Investigators have used a variety of specific research problems, subject samples, and research designs. Previous chapters have emphasized the crucial role of changes in leadership style and organization climate in the implementation of the Scanlon Plan. The importance of increased employee participation in decision making has been stressed in particular. Therefore, the research literature on participative decision making will be reviewed first. Those relatively few studies which have focused directly on the Scanlon Plan as a formal participation/bonus system will then be reviewed, and prescriptions will be offered for future research in this area.

Participative Decision Making (PDM)

The research examining the relationships between participative decision making and employee responses to the job is extensive. No claim is made that the following review of that literature is exhaustive. It does provide an overview of the kind of research which has been conducted in this area and the general results of that research. Those studies that obtained results generally supporting the hypothesis that "participative" or "democratic" leadership practices result in higher productivity or satisfaction or both will be presented first. Those studies which obtained results basically contradictory to this hypothesis and those studies indicating the moderating effect of individual differences on the relationship between leadership practices and employee responses will then be discussed. Only a few of the studies which are representative of the different methodologies employed in this area will be reviewed in any detail.

Several laboratory experiments,[1] small-scale field experiements,[2] field surveys,[3] and large-scale field experiments,[4] have obtained results which, while far from conclusive, have generally supported the hypothesis that participative decision making contributes to favorable employee responses to the job.

A study by Day and Hamblin illustrates the type of laboratory research that supports the participative decision-making hypothesis.[5] This study investigated the effects of "closeness of supervision" in a laboratory simulation of an assembly line. The subjects were freshman and sophomore female college students. Closeness of supervision was manipulated by varying the extent of detail in the instructions given the subjects by their supervisors, who were experimental "stooges."

Positive, statistically significant results were obtained.[6] The average productivity for the group under "close" supervision was twenty-five percent less than that for those under "general" supervision. In addition, aggressive feelings, measured by post-experimental questionnaires, toward both coworkers and the supervisors were higher under close supervision than under general supervision. Day and Hamblin interpreted these results in terms of the expression of aggression as a result of the frustration of ego needs produced by close supervision.

Coch and French's small-scale field experiment is frequently cited in support of the participative decision-making hypothesis.[7] These researchers attempted to extend Lewin's earlier studies on the effectiveness of democratic leadership and group decision[8] as compared to authoritarian leadership and lecture presentation. The site of their study was the main plant of the Harwood Manufacturing Company, located in Marion, Virginia. At the time of the study the plant employed approximately five hundred women and one hundred men, recruited from the rural mountain areas surrounding the town.

A chronic problem facing the management at Harwood was the "resistance" of employees to various changes in job methods and content necessitated by product style changes. This resistance took various forms, from grievances about new rates, high turnover, low efficiency, and restriction of output, to verbal aggression against management following such changes. The experiment was conducted to test the effectiveness of participative decision making in overcoming this problem.

The design included four groups of from seven to eighteen employees each. In the "no participation" group, the change was implemented as

128

usual. The employees were simply informed of the changes involved in factors, such as methods or rates. In the "participation through representation" group, a meeting was held during which the need for change was presented "as dramatically as possible." After agreement was reached that the change was necessary and desirable, this group then chose several operators to help determine the new methods and piece rate and to help train the other operators in the new methods. This procedure was much the same for the two "total participation" groups. Since these groups were smaller, however, all the operators helped determine the new methods and rates.

Immediately after the change all four groups displayed the usual decline in productivity. However, within a few days, striking differences appeared. The no-participation group remained at its immediate post-change low efficiency level for thirty-two days subsequent to the change. There was marked conflict with the methods engineer and hostility against the supervisor. Several grievances were filed, and seventeen percent of the group quit. After thirty-two days this group was broken up, and the individuals were reassigned to jobs scattered throughout the plant. The representative group, on the other hand, showed an unusually good relearning curve. After fourteen days the group's production was slightly above standard; they cooperated with the engineer and their supervisor. There were no grievances filed and no turnover for the first forty days. The total participation group recovered faster and to a higher level of productivity than the representative group. They achieved better than standard production on the second day after the change, and progressed to a sustained level of about fourteen percent above standard. There were no expressions of aggression and no turnover in these groups for the first forty days subsequent to the change.

Finally, two and a half months after the no-participation group had been dispersed, they were reassembled and transferred to a new job using the total participation procedure. In contrast to their earlier behavior, the group quickly recovered from an initial decline in performance, and progressed to fourteen percent above standard within eighteen days. There was no aggression or turnover in the group for nineteen days after the change.

A study by Katz and others provides a good illustration of the survey research that supports the participative decision-making hypothesis.[9] This research was carried out at the home office of the Prudential Life Insurance Company. Twelve section (work group) pairs, which handled the same type of work with the same work organization but differed in their productivity, were compared. All 149 nonsupervisory and 73 supervisory employees were interviewed.

The supervisors of the high-producing sections reported spending more time in supervision *per se*—overseeing and planning the work of their staff —than the low-producing supervisors. The high-producing supervisors were also rated as less "production oriented" and more "employee oriented" and as employing less "close" and more "general" supervision than the low-producing supervisors. "Close" supervision was defined as "the degree to which the supervisor checks up on his employees frequently, gives them detailed and frequent instructions, and, in general, limits the employees' freedom to do the work in their own way." The high-producing supervisors were also coded (blind) by their interviewers as more democratic and less authoritarian than the low-producing supervisors. In addition, the high-producing supervisors reported that they were supervised less closely by their superiors and that they were more satisfied with the degree of their authority and responsibility than the low-producing supervisors.

There have been two large-scale field experiments published which may be cited as generally supporting the hypothesis that participative decision making contributes to favorable employee responses to the job.[10] Both studies were conducted by the Survey Research Center at the University of Michigan and employed Likert's (1961) theory as the conceptual framework for the design of the research.[11]

The Seashore and Bowers study involved an attempt to bring three departments of a manufacturing company's main plant closer to Likert's "participative group" form of organization.[12] An additional two departments served as controls. Changes were implemented through supervisory seminars and discussion sessions, individual counseling sessions, and meetings of employees conducted by line supervisors. Questionnaires were administered in 1958 before the introduction of the change program, in 1959 during the change program, and finally in 1961. The change program was aimed at increasing the following independent variables: the emphasis on group as opposed to individual supervision, the amount of interaction and influence among group members, the degree of participation in decision making and control activities in lower echelons, and the degree of supervisory supportiveness. An analysis of relative changes, based on questionnaire data, indicated that seven of the eleven variables measured changed in the predicted direction. In general, the results for changes in satisfaction, machine efficiency, and absenteeism were positive for the experimental departments and negative for the control departments.

Smith and Jones[13] analyzed data from this study which were not included in the original Seashore and Bowers report. More specifically, they investigated Likert's theory of an interaction influence system, which is hypothesized to intervene between the independent and dependent variables mentioned above and to result in, among other things, increased total control and increased rank-and-file control relative to higher-level control. These increases in control are then said to result in higher motivation and greater consensus and uniformity, which in turn result in increased performance and satisfaction. Questionnaire measures of "general control," plus an index of specific control over pay raises, division of labor, and work methods and standards were analyzed to test this theory. The results provided some support for the total control hypothesis, but no support at all was found for the relative control hypothesis.

For both the general and specific measures, total control increased in the experimental departments and decreased in the control departments. However, according to both the general and the specific measures, positive slope decreased in both the experimental and control departments. An analysis of the changes in control at each hierarchical level revealed that the increases in total control for the experimental department were primarily the result of increases in control attributed to the middle levels of the organization. The authors interpret these results as supporting the notion that participative management may be a means of increasing management's influence as well as, if not more than, that of rank-and-file employees.[14]

The monograph by Marrow and others also describes a change program designed to bring a manufacturing company closer to Likert's participative group model of organization.[15] The change target, the Weldon Manufacturing Company, was acquired by the Harwood owners in 1962. The companies had similar products, but their markets overlapped only slightly. Performance measures were obtained weekly throughout the change program, which lasted about two years. Questionnaire measures were also obtained from random samples of employees in both Harwood and Weldon in 1962, in Weldon in 1963, and again in both Harwood and Weldon in 1964. Pre-post change comparisons were made, with Harwood serving as a "control."

The change process was rather all-encompassing. Many "technical" changes were made in addition to the more "social" ones. On the technical side, new machinery was added, individual jobs were re-engineered, and the work flow was reorganized. On the social side, all the managers down to the first level of supervision were involved in one form or another of sensitivity training; joint problem-solving meetings were held between foremen and workers, and there was a general emphasis on increasing the involvement of lower echelons in decisions affecting their jobs. Other changes included an intensive training program for the operators, the hiring of an additional engineer and a personnel manager, an "earnings development" program, and tougher policies toward absenteeism and chronic low producers.

There can be little doubt that Weldon's performance improved greatly from 1962 to 1964. Some highlights of that improvement included: thirty-two percent increase in return on capital invested, eight percent decrease in make-up pay, twenty-five percent increase in productive efficiency, six percent decrease in monthly turnover rates, and a three percent decrease in daily absenteeism rates. It is impossible, of course, to determine exactly which changes in which combinations resulted in which improvements in performance. Seashore and Bowers, however, on the basis of an analysis of the weekly performance records and the chronology of the various change elements, concluded that they could confidently trace short-run improvements in operator performance to the earnings development program, the weeding out of low producers, the training of supervisors in interpersonal relations, and the joint problem solving between workers and foremen.[16]

The measured changes in attitudes were much less pronounced than the changes in performance. Attitudes toward the company, compensation, and fellow employees improved, but only slightly from 1962 to 1964. In addition, attitudes toward the company and compensation improved more at Harwood than at Weldon during this period. Similarly, there were no significant changes in control, measured by Tannenbaum's procedure,[17] at Weldon, but there were significant increases at Harwood. Finally, all these "negative" results were in striking contrast to the views of management. Self, peer, and superior retroactive change reports, designed to assess the impact of the sensitivity training procedures, produced highly significant changes, as did management ratings on Likert's 43-factor "Profile of Organizational and Performance Characteristics."[18]

NEGATIVE RESULTS

Several studies have failed to support the proposition that participative decision making contributes to favorable employee responses to the job. Several laboratory experiments,[19] field surveys,[20] and field experiments,[21] have obtained results which indicated either no relationship between participative decision making and employee responses or a negative relationship.

An experiment by Shaw, for example, investigated the problem solving performance and satisfaction of four-man groups in different communication networks under democratic and authoritarian leadership. The subjects were male undergraduate college students.[22] As predicted, the problems were solved faster and with fewer errors under authoritarian leadership, but satisfaction was higher under democratic leadership.

Shaw used the concepts "saturation" and independence to predict and interpret his results. Independence refers to the degree of freedom with which a member may operate, and saturation refers to the communication requirements imposed on a group member. Independence is said to correlate positively with efficiency and morale, but after a certain optimal point, saturation tends to counteract these favorable effects. In addition, morale is influenced more by independence than by saturation, while performance is influenced more by saturation than by independence. These concepts are related to leadership style and its effects on performance and satisfaction in the following manner. Authoritarian leadership should decrease independence for most group members and hence decrease morale, and should decrease saturation for all group members and hence increase performance. Democratic leadership, on the other hand, should increase independence for all group members and hence increase morale, and should increase saturation for all group members and hence decrease performance.

A study by Katz and others illustrates the survey research which has failed to support the participative decision-making proposition.[23] In this study, the authors attempted to replicate the findings of their previous study in a markedly different situation. The work groups studied were railroad maintenance crews of the C. & O. Railroad Company. The workers were all men, from small towns or farms, with a median education level of from fifth to eighth grade. Thirty-six pairs of work groups judged comparable on technical work conditions but different on performance were chosen for study. Interviews were conducted with all 298 workers and 72 foremen involved in the study. As in the insurance study, the high-producing foremen were "better able to differentiate their role as leader" and were described by their subordinates as more "employee-oriented" than the low-producing foremen. The insurance study's results concerning closeness of supervision, however, were not replicated. There was no relationship between productivity and closeness of supervision in this study. The authors attempt to explain this inconsistency in terms of the different technologies involved. Methods were sufficiently standardized in the insurance company, they argue, that close supervision could not provide much technical help and represented only a threat and annoyance to the clerks. Since the work of railroad crews was less routine, however, close supervision could contribute to the technical proficiency of the crew, and this contribution apparently "cancelled out" any detrimental effects of close supervision on worker motivation.

Finally, the results of the first large-scale field experiment designed to test the participative decision-making hypothesis failed to support this hypothesis, at least in relation to productivity.[24] The site for this experiement was a large clerical department of the Prudential Life Insurance Company. The rank-and-file decision-making power was increased in two divisions and decreased in two comparable divisions.

The experiment lasted for a year and a half. A questionnaire was administered; six months were spent training supervisors; the experimental conditions were in effect for a year, and then a follow-up questionnaire was administered. The results supported the hypothesis concerning satisfaction. There were significant before-after increases for the "autonomy" program and decreases for the "hierarchical" program for "self-actualization," satisfaction with supervision, and satisfaction with the company, and nonsignificant changes in the predicted direction for job satisfaction. In addition, on several open-ended questions concerning the program itself, the clerks in the autonomy program typically:

> wanted their program to last indefinitely, did not like the other program, felt that the clerks were one of the groups gaining the most from the program and described both positive and negative changes in interpersonal relations among the girls. The clerks in the hierarchically controlled program, on the other hand, most frequently: wanted their program to end immediately, liked the other program, and felt that the company gained the most from their program. Not one single person in the hierarchically controlled program mentioned an improvement in interpersonal relations as a result of this program.[25]

The hypothesis concerning productivity, however, was not confirmed. Both programs resulted in a significant increase in productivity, and the increase in the hierarchical program was significantly greater than that in the autonomy program. As the authors point out, however, the productivity measures were far from perfect and in a sense "stacked against" the autonomy program. The volume of work was not under the control of the units under study. The only way to increase productivity, therefore, was to decrease the number of employees required to do the unit's work. In the hierarchical program, the management simply cut their staff. The clerks in the autonomy program also reduced their numbers—by not replacing employees who left and attempting to find new jobs for employees who wanted to change—but it is certainly to be expected that, for a given unit of time, the hierarchical program would be able to eliminate more employees than the autonomy program. Similarly, the productivity measure employed did not include the reduced investment of managerial time and energy in the autonomy program and the increased investment of these resources in the hierarchical program. The costs of turnover, which was higher in the hierarchical program, were also not included in the performance measures. Finally, Likert has suggested that the differential attitude changes would have resulted in the eventual superiority of the autonomy program had the experiment lasted for a longer period of time.[26]

INDIVIDUAL DIFFERENCES

Several studies have also produced results which may be interpreted as indicating the importance of individual difference variables as moderators of the relationships between leadership practices and employee responses.

Haythorn and others, for example, varied the authoritarianism, as measured by the California F-scale, of leaders and followers within a 2×2 factorial design, such that there were four four-man problem-solving groups within each combination of leader authoritarian (high low) and follower authoritarianism (high-low).[27] The task consisted of a group discussion of a "human relations" film and the composition of a case related to the film. The data collected included observer and subject ratings of various leader and follower behaviors and attitudes.

Several hypotheses, derived mainly from the theory of the authoritarian personality by Adorno and others, were confirmed.[28] Highly authoritarian leaders, for example, were rated as being less equalitarian, less concerned with group approval, more autocratic, and less sensitive to others than less authoritarian leaders. Similarly, leaders with highly authoritarian followers were rated as more autocratic than leaders with less authoritarian followers, and highly authoritarian followers were more satisfied with their appointed leaders and less critical of their groups than less authoritarian followers. On the other hand, contrary to predictions, homogeneous groups were signifi-

135

cantly less satisfied with their leaders than heterogeneous groups, and there were no unambiguous, consistent differences between homogeneous and heterogeneous groups in terms of productivity and morale. Despite these mixed results, the authors interpret their findings as demonstrating the usefulness of conceptualizing leadership as an interaction between the needs and personality structures of both leader and follower.

A small-scale field experiment which is frequently cited as indicating the importance of cultural background as a determinant of employee responses to different leadership practices was conducted by French, Israel, and As in a Norwegian factory.[29] The purpose of this study was to replicate the original Coch and French study,[30] in a different culture using more careful methods and a more precise theory of participation. The general hypothesis predicted positive relationships between participation and productivity, management-worker relations, and job satisfaction. The effects of several conditioning variables were also discussed. Briefly, the authors hypothesized that the above relationships would vary with the perceived legitimacy of participation, and the relevance of the decisions to the dependent variables. The following rationale was given for the general hypotheses. Increases in participation should increase productivity because the decisions involved should be better and because workers should be more motivated to implement them. Participation should relate positively to management-worker relations because the mutual influence involved should lead to greater understanding between the parties and because the implication that the workers are intelligent, competent, and worthy should increase their perception of being valued. Finally, participation should be positively related to job satisfaction because workers' jobs should be improved in ways that are relevant to their needs and because participation should directly satisfy various ego needs.

Nine groups of four workers each were included in the experiment, which involved variations in the participation allowed to the groups in decisions concerning seasonal changes in production. Two of the experimental groups were allowed "moderate participation," which consisted of participation in decisions about the allocation of articles, length of the training, division of labor, and job assignment. The other three experimental groups were given "weak participation," which involved making decisions about the allocation of articles only. The four control groups did not participate in any of these decisions. Questionnaire data revealed that these decisions were of intermediate importance to the workers.

The results revealed no significant differences between the experimental and control groups in productivity. The authors attribute this result to the less than overwhelming importance of the decisions, the low relevance of the decisions to productivity, and to strong group norms restricting productivity. Slight and generally nonsignificant differences in the predicted direction were obtained for the measures of labor-management relations and job satisfaction, and some support was obtained for the postulated conditioning effects of legitimacy and resistance. Especially when the effects of the conditioning variables are considered, the authors interpret their results as being generally consistent with those of the Coch and French study. The literature, however, has emphasized that the Coch and French results were not replicated and that this was probably due to the cultural differences between the Norwegian and Virginia workers involved in the studies.

Vroom's field survey of the interaction between employee needs and personality structure and participation undoubtedly has provided the most clear-cut evidence of the importance of individual differences in determining employee responses to leadership practices.[31] Vroom tested the hypothesis that participation would be more positively related to performance and attitudes for persons low in authoritarianism and for persons with strong independence needs than for persons high in authoritarianism and for persons with weak independence needs.

The data were collected from the supervisory personnel of the two largest "plants" of a delivery company. The need for independence was measured with a sixteen-item questionnaire developed by Tannenbaum and Allport,[32] and authoritarianism was measured with the F-scale. Participation and job attitudes were measured with questionnaire items, and supervisor ratings were used to measure performance. The total sample was divided into three approximately equal groups. Participation was correlated with attitudes and performance for the total sample and for those within each group. The results strongly supported the hypotheses. Participation was correlated positively and significantly with both attitudes and performance for the total sample. Both correlations, however, were higher for supervisors high in need of independence than for supervisors low in independence. In addition, both correlations were lower for high authoritarian supervisors than for low authoritarian supervisors.

Finally, Tannenbaum and Allport[33] used data collected in the Morse and Reimer[34] study to test the hypothesis that personality characteristics and organizational structure, in this case the "hierarchical" and "autonomy" change programs, should interact to determine work-related attitudes. Essentially, their hypothesis, derived from Allport's event-structure theory,[35] was that individuals with personalities "suited" to the different experimental programs would have more favorable attitudes toward these programs than individuals with less "suited" personalities. The specific conceptual and operational definitions of personality "trend structures" and their "suitedness" to the experimental programs were derived from Allport's theory, which is rather esoteric and beyond the scope of a few paragraphs. In more familiar language, however, an individual's personality is "suited" to a given social structure to the extent that that structure provides him with the opportunity to achieve his important goals or to satisfy his dominant motives. Twenty-six such motives were identified as being relevant to the experimental programs. The importance of the motives for each of the subjects was measured by Likert-type questionnaire items, and three judges estimated the extent to which the different programs would provide satisfaction for each of the motives. The attitudes measured included desired length of the program, satisfaction with the way the program operates, and two measures of degree of liking for the program.

Although the differences were not extremely large, nor always statistically significant, especially when each program was considered by itself, the results generally confirmed the hypothesis. When the data for the two programs were combined, three of the four attitude measures yielded the predicted differences significant at the .05 level. The differences for the fourth measure, "satisfaction with the way the program operates," were significant at the .10 level.

SUMMARY

In summary, there is a good deal of support from a variety of different research designs, measurement procedures, and subject samples for the hypothesis that participative decision making contributes to favorable employee responses to the job. It seems quite clear from this research that participative decision making *can* contribute to organizational effectiveness, individual performance, and job satisfaction. The research conducted to date indicates that participative decision making has, in fact, resulted in such favorable outcomes in many instances.

On the other hand, a few studies have failed to support this hypothesis, and some evidence indicates that the relationship between participative decision making and employee responses may be affected by individual differences, such that certain types of employees may not respond as positively as others. Unfortunately, the research conducted to date, while suggestive, does not provide many firmly established guidelines concerning which employees under which circumstances are more or less likely to respond favorably to participative decision making. We also know very little about which types of managers are more or less willing and able to manage in a participative manner. In addition, the question of the permanence of these individual differences has not yet been systematically studied. It may well be, for example, that certain types of employees or managers are more likely to respond negatively to participation initially, but these predispositions may change through training, experience with the participative process, and socialization. Suggestions for remedying these deficiencies in our knowledge about the participative decision-making process are offered later in this chapter.

The Scanlon Plan

Several studies have reported that the implementation of the Scanlon Plan has resulted in increased productivity and employee earnings. These studies also frequently attributed improvements in such variables as the climate of labor-management relations, employee attitudes toward the company, acceptance of change, and interdepartmental cooperation to the Scanlon Plan. In addition, there have been a few published reports of cases in which the Scanlon Plan has apparently failed, or at least been abandoned, and some attention has been devoted to the examination of variables which might affect the results achieved through the adoption of the Plan.

POSITIVE RESULTS

The first published articles on the Scanlon Plan reported the experiences of the Adamson Company, a small organization that manufactured steel storage tanks.[36] The company had been organized by the Steelworkers Organizing Committee in 1937. Management had not resisted the organization, and the relationship between the union and management was stable and peaceful. A labor-management production committee established during the war to facilitate joint efforts to increase productivity had functioned with some success. After a joint examination of various types of profit-sharing plans by both labor and management, the Scanlon Plan was installed in January 1945. Although the company had been a consistent profit maker and had paid the highest wages in the community and industry, the installation of the Plan was followed by dramatic increases in productivity, profits, and employee earnings. In the first year under the Plan, profits increased 150 percent, and the employees received bonuses equal to 41 percent of their base wages. During the second year, profits increased almost 100 percent, and employee bonuses averaged 54 percent of base wages.[37]

Several articles have described the experiences of the LaPointe Machine Tool Company with the Scanlon Plan.[38] The LaPointe Company, which employed approximately 350 people at the time of the installation of the Scanlon Plan, manufactured machine cutting tools. The plant was organized by the United Steelworkers in 1945 and experienced an eleven-week strike one year later. Approximately one-third of the employees were covered with a piece-work incentive system. The problems associated with this system—inequities in rates and earnings, restriction of output, friction between direct and indirect employees—led the local union president to propose the adoption of the Scanlon Plan. The Plan was investigated by a joint labor-management committee and was installed in December 1947. In the first two years under the Plan, 513 suggestions were received, only 65 of which were rejected. During this same period, bonuses averaging 18 percent of base wages were earned and profits reportedly increased. Improvements were also reported in areas such as delivery times, grievance rates, and quality. Experienced and skilled employees reportedly began for the first time to share the "tricks of their trade" and to help train new employees.

Tait briefly outlined the early experiences of the Stromberg-Carlson Company with the Scanlon Plan.[39] In 1949 the company was losing money, and the employees, who were represented by an independent union, agreed to forego a wage increase because of the company's financial difficulties. During the discussions which resulted in this agreement, the company president had indicated that he was interested in exploring some form of profit-sharing plan to replace the individual piece-work system then in effect. After several months of study by a joint labor-management committee, the Scanlon Plan was installed in July 1950. During the first year and a half under the Plan, 1,300 suggestions were received, half of which were accepted. Approximately thirty percent were rejected, and another twenty percent were still pending further investigation. During the first six months, bonuses averaging twelve percent of base wages were earned, and the company reportedly returned to a profit-making basis. The following year, however, the "bottom fell out of the market" for one of the company's three divisions, and no bonuses were earned. According to Tait, this situation was difficult because volume and profits in the other divisions were higher than ever before, and many employees felt that they should be receiving bonuses. On the other hand, Tait reported that people began to understand the importance of the welfare of the total company and did not want to return to the former piece-work system.

Puckett studied the changes in productivity following the installation of the Scanlon Plan in ten different cases.[40] The ten cases involved nine companies and eleven plants. One organization applied the Plan separately in two plants, and another organization included two plants under the same measurement. These cases were reportedly chosen for study on the basis of the ease with which available data could be translated into reliable estimates of changes in productivity. Puckett claimed that the firms could be considered a representative sample of the situations in which the Plan had been installed.

According to Puckett, the firms studied represented a wide variety of environments and circumstances. Three of the firms produced consumer goods, three manufactured capital goods, one made parts for consumer items, and two made finished products for use in construction in public institutions. The elasticity of demand for the products of these firms was reportedly high for half of the firms and low for the other half. Employees were represented by no union in one case, by an independent union in one case, and by affiliates of national unions in eight cases. The number of employees ranged from 30 in the smallest plant to 1,200 in the largest plant. Three plants had fewer than 100 employees, five plants had from 101 to 400 employees, and two plants had from 1,001 to 1,200 employees. The labor content of the sales value of production ranged from a low of ten percent to a high of sixty percent. The firms also varied widely in profitability prior to the installation of the Plan. Two of the firms had been exceptionally profitable prior to adoption of the Plan, three firms had better than average profits for their industries, two had average profitability, and two had been faced with severe financial losses and the possibility of liquidation. Similarly, the types of production process varied from mass production to job-shop situations, and the skill levels ranged from highly skilled machining and tool making to low skilled manual operations.

Productivity changes were measured by comparing the ratio of the sales value of production to total payroll costs in the first two years of operation under the Scanlon Plan with the ratio of these two variables in the base period. In each case, the base period covered at least one full year. Although the procedures were not described in detail, adjustments were made for the effects of changes in variables which could distort the labor cost ratio as a measure of productivity. More specifically, adjustments were made for the effects of changes in prices, wages, technology, product mix, new products, fixed elements of the work force, overtime hours, and "farmed-out" work brought back into the plant. The results of this analysis are presented in Table 8.

Productivity increased for the two-year period in each of the ten cases. For the first year following the installation of the Plan, the productivity increases ranged from a low of 6.8 percent to a high of 38.7 percent, with an average of 28.1 percent. In the second year, the improvement ranged from 10.9 percent to 49.4 percent, with an average of 23.7 percent. The average increase for the two-year period was 28.1 percent. In addition, although no data were reported, Puckett claimed that none of the environmental variables studied correlated with the degree of improvement in productivity.

TABLE 8

Productivity in 10 Scanlon Companies*

Company	First-Year Relative Efficiency	Second-Year Relative Efficiency	Two-Year Average-Relative Efficiency (Unweighted)
	(1)	(2)	(3)
A	14.9	10.9	12.9
B	21.9	12.7	17.3
C	16.7	13.2	15.0
D	36.7	29.3	33.0
E	28.9	49.4	39.2
F	32.9	42.9	37.9
G	38.7	25.1	31.9
H	14.1	16.5	15.3
I	12.9	23.2	18.1
J	6.8	13.7	10.3
Average (Unweighted)	22.5	23.7	23.1

*From Lesieur (1958), p. 113.

The previously cited studies have all described the experiences of companies during the first few years following the installation of the Scanlon Plan. In contrast, Lesieur and Puckett described the experiences of three organizations in which the Scanlon Plan had been in effect for more than ten years.[41] According to them, each of the three cases represented different situations and problems, and together the cases included "just about all" of the kinds of problems which are typically encountered by industrial organizations.

The first case analyzed was the Atwood Vacuum Machine Company, a family-owned organization, which operated six plants and employed over 2,000 people. The employees were represented by three independent unions. All employees, including the president of the company, participated in the Scanlon Plan, which at the time of the study had been in effect for fourteen years. Atwood produced automotive parts for all the major automobile manufacturers and also had a general product division which manufactured products such as trailer hitches, brake actuating systems, and trailer hot-water heaters. These products were manufactured on a high volume, mass production basis. An individual incentive system was dropped when the Scanlon Plan was adopted.

During the fourteen years following the installation of the Scanlon Plan, over 25,000 suggestions were submitted. Annual bonuses ranged from a high of 20 percent of payroll to a low of 5 percent. Bonuses were earned in 87 percent of the 187 periods of operation, and the highest monthly bonus was approximately 26 percent. In 1969 the ratio of total payroll costs to the sales value of production was within 0.5 percent of the ratio at the time the plan had been installed. According to Lesieur and Puckett, there had been a close correlation between bonuses paid and annual profits.

The second case described by Lesieur and Puckett was the Parker Pen Company, which had used the Scanlon Plan in its manufacturing division located in Janesville, Wisconsin, for fourteen years. Approximately 1,000 employees were covered by the Plan. Two international unions, the United Rubber Workers and the International Association of Machinists, were involved. Parker manufactures writing instruments on a high-volume production basis. The market is a highly competitive one. An individual incentive system was dropped when the Scanlon Plan was installed.

Under the Scanlon Plan annual bonuses ranged from a high of 20 percent to a low of 5.5 percent. Bonuses were earned in 84 percent of the 168 months during which the Plan was in effect. The highest monthly bonus was approximately 30 percent. The correlation between bonuses paid and division profits was reportedly excellent. Prior to the installation of the Plan, labor costs had risen so much that close to 50 percent of the company's product was being manufactured outside of the Janesville plant. In 1969 better than 80 percent of the product was manufactured in this plant. The ratio of total payroll costs to the sales value of production had risen by slightly over one percentage point since the Scanlon Plan had been adopted.

The final case discussed by Lesieur and Puckett was the Pfaudler Company, a manufacturer of chemical, pharmaceutical, food-manufacturing, and brewery equipment, in which the Scanlon Plan had been in effect for seventeen years. Approximately 750 employees were covered by the Plan. Two unions were involved, the United Steelworkers of America and the Coppersmithing Branch of Sheet Metal Trades. Pfaudler's production process was described as a "large job shop," in that much of its product is engineered and tailored to customer specification.

Annual bonuses ranged from 17.5 percent of base wages to 3 percent of wages. Bonuses were earned in 88 percent of the 204 months during which the Plan was in effect. The highest monthly bonus earned was approximately 22 percent. The ratio of payroll costs to the sales value of production was substantially lower in 1969 than it had been when the Plan was installed, but this was primarily because corporate personnel had moved to a new corporate headquarters and no longer participated in the Plan. Although no specific data were reported, Lesieur and Puckett claim that thousands of suggestions for improvement had been submitted, many of which had produced substantial savings in cost or improved quality.

According to Lesieur and Puckett, the primary benefits of the Scanlon Plan for these organizations included increased efficiency and productivity, increased labor-management cooperation, and increased employee willingness to accept technological change. Unfortunately, the authors did not provide sufficient data to enable the reader to draw his own conclusions about the effects of the Scanlon Plan in these organizations. The authors imply that over ten years of consistent bonus earnings and wage increases "in line with area and national patterns" in connection with no, or minimal, increases in the ratio of labor costs to the sales value of production are evidence of increased productivity and efficiency. In the absence of information about changes in prices, however, these data are actually ambiguous with respect to changes in productivity. The Parker Pen Company apparently was unable to raise prices appreciably, but no information was provided about changes in prices for Atwood or Pfaudler.

The studies discussed thus far have all reported favorable results from the installation of the Scanlon Plan. Although these studies provide valuable case material, they offer little in the way of unambiguous data. Taken as a whole, these studies seem to indicate that employee suggestions, productivity, and earnings increased substantially in the first few years following the installation of the Scanlon Plan in several organizations. Similarly, the Lesieur and Puckett study indicates that at least three organizations, each with over ten years' experience with the Scanlon Plan, have paid consistent bonuses and increases in wages without experiencing appreciable increases in the ratio of payroll costs to the sales value of production. In addition, these studies provide qualitative evidence that the Scanlon Plan has resulted in improved labor-management cooperation, more favorable attitudes toward the company, and increased acceptance of change. On the other hand, few quantitative data have been reported with respect to these variables.

NEGATIVE RESULTS

In addition to the studies which have reported favorable results, three articles have described cases in which the Scanlon Plan reportedly failed to yield results consistent with the expectations of the parties involved. Gilson and Lefcowitz, for example, described a case in which the Scanlon Plan was abandoned by a small, family-owned firm engaged in the manufacture of ceramic gifts.[42] The firm employed approximately fifty to eighty employees, who were represented by a C.I.O.-affiliated union. The work force reportedly consisted primarily of women, minority group members, and "displaced persons." The Scanlon Plan was adopted in response to a union demand for an "adequate incentive system." Apparently little effort was devoted to analyzing the Plan's underlying philosophy or the implications of this philosophy for changes in attitudes and behavior by management and labor. After one year of operation, the Plan was replaced by an individual incentive system at the request of the employees and their union. Under the Plan, direct labor cost as a proportion of manufacturing cost had decreased from 67.5 percent to 52.5 percent, and the workers had received bonuses amounting to an extra week's pay, but these results, according to the authors, did not measure up to the participants' expectations.

Gilson and Lefcowitz attributed the Plan's failure to the following factors:

1. The basically autocratic management did not really want participation, and the union was too weak to press the issue or to accept the responsibilities inherent in participation.
2. There was a lack of mutual trust between the workers and management.
3. The Plan was never adequately explained to the workers.
4. Little information on such items as payroll costs, production goals, or the quality of production was provided for the lower organization levels.
5. The Production Committee meetings focused on grievances and complaints against management rather than on production problems.
6. No one assumed the role of "evangelist" in encouraging everyone to strive for improvement.

Jehring described a case in which the Scanlon Plan was abandoned in favor of a profit-sharing plan.[43] The company involved was a small family-owned manufacturer of household fixtures. A large percentage of the employees were women from small farm communities. The employees were not represented by a union. The Scanlon Plan had been installed in 1956, and by 1961 the bonuses had diminished to practically nothing, despite the fact that the company had expanded and profits had increased substantially. This situation apparently resulted from the fact the adjustments had not been made in the ratio to reflect changes in the product mix, which over the years resulted in a large percentage of production requiring substantially more labor than that allowed in the ratio. Earning a bonus under such circumstances was practically impossible. Jehring reported that the formula had not been changed because the accountant felt that the bookkeeping work would have been too difficult.

Gray reported his analysis of the factors resulting in the failure of the Scanlon Plan at the Linwood plant of the Pressed Steel Company.[44] The Pressed Steel Company is a large, independent body producer for the auto industry located in Great Britain. The Scanlon Plan was adopted by the Linwood plant, which employed 6,000 people, in October 1963, and was abandoned in February 1966. Gray's study dealt primarily with the first year of the Plan's operation.

Prior to the installation of the Scanlon Plan, a piecework system had been in effect. This system had resulted in wide discrepancies in earnings opportunities and frequent disputes over wage inequities. The management style at Linwood had been considered highly authoritarian by the workers, by new managers imported from other parts of the parent company, and by

146

the consultants who introduced the Plan. According to Gray, however, by the time the Plan had been adopted, changes in management had resulted in a much less authoritarian system.

For the first six months under the Plan, bonuses averaged 12 percent of base wages. During the next six months, however, bonuses dropped to an average of 3.23 percent. Subsequent bonus earnings apparently were quite negligible. In addition, according to Gray, the Scanlon Plan failed to cure restrictive practices, reduce absenteeism, or improve labor-management relations. To the contrary, in Gray's opinion, the Plan either contributed to existing problems or created new ones.

Gray's analysis of the events involved in this case led him to conclude that the Plan's failure resulted from "a combination of technological and economic factors, which, in connection with a characteristic of the payment system so affected vital job interests that it outweighed the sense of common purpose."[45] More specifically, Gray reported that the change from piece-work to the Scanlon Plan increased the need for frequent manpower redeployment within and between departments in response to continually changing production schedules. This need for manpower flexibility was particularly great in several key departments. The workers in the departments most affected, however, greatly resented redeployment, which represented a threat to established patterns of status and work relationships, and these conflicting interests prevented a sense of common purpose from developing.

In addition, Gray reported that he found no evidence in this case to support the frequent assertion that the failure of the Scanlon Plan is due to management authoritarianism or a lack of commitment to the philosophy of the Plan. This conclusion was based on his analysis of: (1) the relationship of supervisory style to departmental suggestion rates and (2) changes in plant-wide turnover rates subsequent to the Plan's adoption. The first analysis revealed no relationship between suggestion rates and the reported authoritarianism of supervisors in the Plant's twelve departments. In addition, Gray interpreted the fact that plant-wide turnover dropped significantly following the installation of the Scanlon Plan as indicating that the Plan failed despite changes in management style in the direction of a more participative approach.

The rather indirect data on which Gray based his conclusions concerning the failure of the Scanlon Plan at Linwood are, of course, far from unambiguous. The "correlation" between departmental suggestion rates and supervisory style was actually a comparison of two departments. In addition, no quantitative data were used to measure leadership style. Rather, the departments were classified as more or less "authoritarian" on the basis of Gray's subjective assessment of their general reputations. Similarly, turnover rate is at best a highly indirect measure of management style. Gray defends these procedures on the grounds that authoritarianism and management style are subjective concepts and are consequently difficult to measure objectively. Measurement is a problem, of course, for most of the variables of interest to social scientists. On the other hand, a good deal of research cited earlier in this chapter indicates that it is possible to measure leadership style using systematic, quantitative methods.

Even if Gray's conclusions concerning the causes of the failure of the Scanlon Plan in this case are accepted, the question of their generality remains unanswered. In one of the other two published reports of Scanlon Plan failures, Gilson and Lefcowitz reached the opposite conclusion concerning the effects of management style.[46] That is, they reported that, in the case they studied, management's unwillingness to change its basically autocratic style contributed to the lack of positive results achieved by the Scanlon Plan.

MEDIATING FACTORS

Finally, two articles have examined variables which might affect the results achieved through the adoption of the Scanlon Plan by comparing the experiences or organizations which have implemented the Plan with varying degrees of success.[47] On the basis of two "fragmentary field studies" and their analysis of previously published cases, Strauss and Sayles discussed several factors which they considered necessary for the success of the Scanlon Plan.[48] First of all, they concluded that the success of the Scanlon Plan requires greatly increased interaction among all the parties involved. According to them, if this does not occur, either the union will use the Plan as a means of expressing their dissatisfaction with management's inefficiency or the union officers will become alienated from the rank-and-file workers.

Secondly, management has to be willing to accept substantial criticism from lower organization levels, as well as the usual criticisms from above. Middle management and staff personnel are particularly threatened in this respect, because they are not involved in the committee activity and some of their previous duties may be eliminated. The reactions of first-level supervisors are also crucial in this respect. They may view too many good suggestions as reflecting poorly on their competence as managers and therefore may stifle good suggestions.

In addition, Strauss and Sayles contended that the channels of communication must be expanded considerably to include production and cost data, and that the company must be able to increase sales to the extent of any increases in production if the Scanlon Plan is to succeed. Finally, according to these authors, the larger the company, the more important it becomes for each department to have its own production or efficiency goals in conjunction with the overall plant goals.

In a similar article, Helfgott discussed several factors which he considered necessary for the successful implementation of the Scanlon Plan.[49] Helfgott based his conclusions on an analysis of the previously published literature and on his comparison of the experiences of six organizations which had adopted the Scanlon Plan with varying degrees of success. The six organizations ranged in size from three hundred to a few thousand employees and were engaged in different types of manufacturing. Two of the organizations had abandoned the Plan after two years. Two organizations had retained the Plan for periods of eight to ten years, and two organizations had recently adopted the Plan as a solution to problems threatening the existence of the plants.

Helfgott provided no quantitative data, but his analysis of the literature and the experiences of these six organizations led him to conclude that the Scanlon Plan's applicability to American industry is limited by several factors. More specifically, according to him, the successful implementation of the Scanlon Plan requires the following factors:

1. *Assurance that regular bonuses can be paid.* If the Plan does not produce high bonuses, the morale of employees will be adversely affected, and the Plan will fail.
2. *A basic need for the Plan,* such as severe financial difficulty or an intolerable incentive system. Only under such circumstances, can the necessary labor-management unity and cooperation be developed.
3. *Full, enthusiastic support of the basic concepts and principles of the Plan* by top management, management in general, and union officials. It is the zeal of the Scanlon Plan supporters and their enthusiasm which makes the Plan work. Without this support, employees lose interest in the Plan. In general, gaining the full support of management requires a thorough reorientation of management thinking.

Management must be willing to encourage union participation and share some vital managerial functions with employee representatives.

4. *Complete cooperation of all employees.* All employees must seriously work at reducing costs and increasing efficiency through the suggestion system. If any group holds back, the Plan will necessarily fail.

SUMMARY

Few unambiguous conclusions concerning the effects of the Scanlon Plan can be drawn from the research conducted to date. This state of affairs is hardly surprising, given the nature of research in the area. The bulk of this research has consisted of description and qualitative analysis of the experiences of small samples (one to ten) of organizations with the Plan. Quantitative research methods have been the exception rather than the rule. As for participative decision making in general, the research conducted to date does indicate that the Scanlon Plan *can* result in improved organizational effectiveness and individual performance and satisfaction. Increased productivity and employee earnings during the first few years following the installation of the Plan have been documented for several organizations. In addition, a few organizations have reportedly paid consistent bonuses and wage increases without experiencing appreciable increases in the ratio of labor costs to the sales value of production for over ten years subsequent to the adoption of the Scanlon Plan.[50] These studies have also typically reported that the Scanlon Plan has resulted in improved labor-management cooperation, more favorable attitudes toward the company, and increased acceptance of change; however, few quantitative data have been reported with respect to these variables.

On the other hand, the experiences of several organizations with the Scanlon Plan were unfavorable enough to result in its abandonment. Little is known, however, about the specific variables which might facilitate or hinder the effectiveness of the Plan. The authors of most of the studies in the area have offered conclusions concerning the factors necessary for the successful implementation of the Plan, but, given the nature of the data from which such conclusions have been drawn, it would be more appropriate to consider them hypotheses to be investigated by future research.

Prescriptions for Future Research

As indicated in the preceding review of the research on the Scanlon Plan, one of the primary problems with this research is the lack of systematic, quantitative data. Qualitative data is valuable, to be sure. Such data can provide insights and awareness which are frequently difficult to derive from "cold, hard numbers." However, scientific research requires the collection of quantitative data in order to facilitate objectivity, in order to facilitate precise, analytical conceptualization, and in order to insure precision and clarity in communicating research results. In addition, as previous chapters have indicated, the Scanlon Plan is a complex system of interdependent elements, rather than a single, unidimensional variable. The effectiveness of the Plan is, therefore, very likely beyond simple proof or disproof. Consequently, the most appropriate direction for future research should involve the systematic, quantitative investigation of intervening and moderating variables which might mediate the effects of efforts to implement the Plan.

In a recent review of the literature on participative decision making (PDM), Lowin presented a model of the relationships among PDM and organizational, situational, and individual difference variables which should be extremely useful in directing future research on the Scanlon Plan.[51] Lowin's model is basically a model of organization change, the primary emphasis of which is on the conditions—that is, the organizational, situational, and individual difference variables—that may facilitate or hinder change toward more PDM-oriented systems of organization such as the Scanlon Plan.

Lowin's model places heavy emphasis on the attitudes of managers and subordinates toward PDM, which is defined as "a mode of organizational operations in which decisions as to activities are arrived at by the very persons who are to execute those decisions. PDM is contrasted with the conventional hierarchical mode of operations in which decision and action functions are segregated in the authority structure." It is assumed that: (1) managers and subordinates hold reliable and consistent attitudes about the desirability and usefulness of PDM; (2) the PDM attitudes of a given superior and his subordinates are congruent; and (3) given the opportunity, such attitudes result in behaviors and interactions supportive of or inimical to PDM.

Within this framework, the deliberate induction of a PDM program is viewed as an attempt to shift a stable social system from one position on the PDM-HIER dimension to another. The experimenter or change agent must therefore "unfreeze" the current social system and alter the attitudes, behaviors, and interactions of the parties involved at least to the extent necessary for the successful development of PDM. If such "unfreezing" is not achieved, negative attitudes toward PDM will abort the change effort irrespective of the latent value of PDM. Even if the change agent is able to obtain temporary behavioral compliance with his demands for PDM, however, permanent changes in the organization require major shifts in attitudes, which can be achieved only to the extent that the needs of employees and the organization are satisfied more under the PDM system than under the conventional hierarchical system. If the needs of either employees or the organization are not met more effectively by PDM, the program will ultimately be rejected, and the organization will revert to a hierarchical system.

Lowin suggests the employee and organizational needs which may be met by PDM.

EMPLOYEE NEEDS LIKELY MET BY PDM

Ego Needs. Employee needs such as the needs for achievement, autonomy, power, and self-actualization are likely to be satisfied through PDM.

Financial Needs. The connection between PDM and financial rewards is frequently rather indirect. Under the Scanlon Plan, however, improvements in organizational effectiveness resulting from PDM activities result in increased financial awards.

Closure and the Sense of Participation. In a PDM system, the employee is more fully aware of his role in a complex system, and the meaningfulness of his daily activities is enriched.

ORGANIZATIONAL AND MANAGEMENT NEEDS LIKELY MET BY PDM

Organizational Performance. Managers are primarily concerned with improving organizational performance. To the extent that PDM improves organizational performance, therefore, it should contribute to the satisfaction of managers' needs for ego and financial rewards. PDM may contribute to improved performance through the following mechanisms.

Improvements in Technical and Administrative Systems. The firsthand experience of employees with technological and administrative systems may provide them with knowledge and insights not normally available to managers and technical staff. Therefore, PDM may improve the quality of decisions by increasing the validity of information used in the decision-making process.

Social Pressures to Implement Decisions. Employees may be subject to increased social pressure from both peers and superiors for the implementation of decisions in which they have participated. Under PDM, the employee may be under increased social pressure not to renege on an earlier stand.

Shared Goals. PDM should increase commonality of information and perceived goal interdependence which contribute to internalization of organizational goals.

Changes in Manager Behavior. Although the traditional focus in the PDM literature has been on subordinate motivation and behavior, PDM may also pressure management and staff to more carefully consider their decisions, by subjecting them to more critical review than under HIER.

On the basis of this analysis of the general conditions necessary for a successful program of change toward PDM and the organizational, managerial, and employee needs potentially met by PDM, Lowin's model specified the following more specific hypotheses concerning the parameters of PDM effectiveness:

PDM effectiveness varies directly with . . .
. the extent of PDM activities
. the relevance and importance of PDM activities
. the visibility of PDM activities
. the difficulty of activities settled through PDM
. the extent of dyadic and group social pressure
. the clarity of PDM-generated goals
. the degree of coupling of financial rewards with PDM activities
. the amount of useful information available exclusively to subordinates.
. the extent of subordinate control over productivity
. the number of administrative levels subsumed by the Program.

PDM effectiveness varies inversely with . . .
. the amount of useful information not available to the subordinate
. the urgency of decisions.

The implications of Lowin's model for future research on the Scanlon Plan are relatively clear. Anecdotes and testimonials, while interesting and frequently enlightening, are unlikely to add significantly to scientific knowledge about the Scanlon Plan. Similarly, simplistic hypotheses concerning the effects of PDM programs in general and the Scanlon Plan in particular are undoubtedly too gross to be proved or disproved. Future research should emphasize the systematic, quantitative investigation of variables, such as those outlined by Lowin's model, which are likely to mediate the effectiveness of the Scanlon Plan. Longitudinal studies, in which the complex relationships among the variables of interest can be traced over time, should be particularly fruitful.

NOTES TO CHAPTER 6

Note: For complete references see pp. 192–97.

1. Day and Hamblin, 1964; Lewin, Lippitt, and White, 1939; Lewin, 1947; Missumi, 1959.
2. Coch and French, 1948; Fleishman, 1965; Lawrence and Smith, 1955; Lawler and Hackman, 1969; Levine and Butler, 1952; Strauss, 1955.
3. Backman et al., 1968; Backman et al., 1966; Bowers, 1964; Indik et al., 1961; Katz et al., 1950; Smith and Ari, 1964; Smith and Tannenbaum, 1963; Tannenbaum and Smith, 1964; Yuchtman, 1968.
4. Marrow et al., 1967; Seashore and Bowers, 1963.
5. Day and Hamblin, 1964.
6. "Statistically significant" means unlikely to have resulted from chance.
7. Coch and French, 1948.
8. Lewin et al., 1939; Lewin, 1947.
9. Katz et al., 1950
10. Marrow, Bowers, and Seashore, 1967; Seashore and Bowers, 1963.
11. Seashore and Bowers, 1963.
12. Smith and Jones, 1968.
14. March and Simon, 1958; Tannenbaum, 1968.
15. Marrow et al., 1967.
16. Seashore and Bowers, 1963.
17. Tannenbaum, 1968.
18. Likert, 1967.
19. McCurdy and Eber, 1953; Sales, 1964; Shaw, 1955; Spector and Suttell, 1957.
20. Katz et al., 1951; Tosi, 1970.
21. Morse and Reimer, 1956.
22. Shaw, 1955.
23. Katz et al., 1951.
24. Morse and Reimer, 1956.
25. Ibid.
26. Likert, 1967.
27. Haythorn et al., 1956.
28. Adorno el al., 1950.
29. French, Israel, and As, 1960.
30. Coch and French, 1948.
31. Vroom, 1959.
32. Tannenbaum and Allport, 1956.
33. Ibid.
34. Morse and Reimer, 1956.
35. Allport, 1954.
36. Chamberlain, 1946; Scanlon, 1948.
37. Scanlon, 1948.

38. Davenport, 1950; Doud, 1955; Lesieur, 1952; Schultz and Crisara, 1952.
39. Tait, 1952.
40. Puckett, 1958.
41. Lesieur and Puckett, 1969.
42. Gilson and Lefcowitz, 1957.
43. Jehring, 1967.
44. Gray, 1971.
45. Ibid., p. 301.
46. Gilson and Lefcowitz, 1957.
47. Helfgott, 1962; Strauss and Sayles, 1957.
48. Strauss and Sayles, 1957.
49. Helfgott, 1962.
50. Lesieur and Puckett, 1969.
51. Lowin, 1968.

CHAPTER 7

Recent Research
on the Scanlon Plan

IN RECENT YEARS the Scanlon Plan Associates (SPA) and the Psychology Department of Michigan State University have jointly sponsored several research projects like those called for in the preceding chapter. Several of these studies will be reviewed here in order to give the reader concrete illustrations of the type of research which must be conducted if the state of scientific knowledge about the Scanlon Plan is to progress. Six studies will be reviewed. All the studies were conducted in organizations which have or at one time had the Scanlon Plan. Most of these organizations are active members of the Scanlon Plan Associates. The participation of these organizations in this research and their membership in SPA is tangible evidence that practical, "hard-nosed" businessmen can appreciate and actively support social science research. In fact, several executives in these organizations actively participated in the planning of much of the research. In a very real sense, this research would not have been possible without the existence of SPA and the cooperation of its member companies. The first study to be reviewed investigated the effects of management attitudes toward participative decision making and toward employees on the implementation of the Scanlon Plan. The other studies examined the role of participative decision making in the Scanlon Plan, employee perceptions of the Plan, and the effects of individual differences in personal background, needs, and values in structuring employee responses to job and organizational characteristics, such as participative decision making (PDM).

Management Attitudes and the Scanlon Plan

According to Lowin, the primary determinants of the successful implementation of a PDM program such as the Scanlon Plan are the attitudes of the individuals involved toward each other and toward the PDM process.[1] The theoretical and case literature on the Scanlon Plan also emphasizes the important role of attitudes, especially management attitudes, in the successful implementation of the Scanlon Plan. More specifically, Lowin's model and the theoretical literature on the Scanlon Plan predict that the Plan will be retained only in those organizations in which managers hold positive attitudes toward subordinates and toward PDM. The case study literature on the Scanlon Plan, with the exception of Gray, supports this proposition,[2] but no previous studies have quantitatively measured management attitudes. Therefore, a study was designed to investigate the relationship between management attitudes and retention of the Scanlon Plan.[3]

METHOD

Sample. Questionnaire data were collected from managers at all levels of the hierarchy in eighteen manufacturing organizations which had attempted to implement the Scanlon Plan. All the organizations had at least two years' experience with the Plan. Ten of these organizations were currently operating under the Scanlon Plan and were active members of the Scanlon Plan Associates. Eight of the organizations had abandoned the plan. The organizations that retained the Plan ranged in size from 23 to 3,000 employees, and the organizations which had abandoned it had from 66 to 700 employees. Eight of the organizations which retained the Plan and six of those which had abandoned it were located in cities with populations under 100,000. Usable returns were received from 205 (79.5 percent) of the 258 managers to whom questionnaires were distributed. Of these, 133 were from managers of firms with continuing Scanlon Plans, and 72 were from managers of firms which had abandoned the Plan.

Questionnaire. The questionnaire used was developed by R. E. Miles to assess attitudes related to his human resources—human relations model of

157

management style.[4] The questionnaire had two main sections. In the first section, the respondent was asked to indicate on seven-point scales the extent to which rank-and-file employees, his immediate subordinates, people at his own hierarchical level, and people at the level of his superior possess the following traits: judgment, creativity, responsibility, dependability, pride in performance, alertness, initiative, self-confidence, long-range perspective, and willingness to change. "Confidence in employee" scores were computed by subtracting the respondent's ratings of rank-and-file employees from his ratings of employees at his own level. The second section consists of twenty-seven five-point, Likert-type items, for which the respondent was asked to indicate his agreement with statements concerning the desirability and usefulness of PDM. More specifically, this section contains nine questions concerning each of the following participative policies:

1. Subordinates should be encouraged to participate in decision making in their own departments.
2. Each subordinate should be allowed to participate in the setting of his own performance goals.
3. Subordinates should be allowed to use their ingenuity in modifying and adapting the techniques and procedures required in their jobs.

The respondent was asked to indicate his general approval of these policies and his opinion of the impact that these policies would have on morale and on performance if they were applied at: (1) the lowest level in the organization, (2) with his immediate subordinates, and (3) at his own level.

RESULTS AND DISCUSSION

The mean "confidence in employees" scores for managers in continuing and discontinued Scanlon Plan companies are presented in Table 9. Since these scores were derived by subtracting the respondents' ratings of rank-and-file employees from their ratings of employees at their own level, higher scores indicate relatively less confidence in rank-and-file employees. Inspection of the results reported in Table 9 indicates that there are significant differences in confidence in employees between managers in continuing and discontinued Scanlon Plan firms. As hypothesized, the managers in companies which have abandoned the Scanlon Plan perceive rank-and-file employees to demonstrate less judgment, creativity, responsibility, dependability, pride in performance, alertness, initiative, self-confidence, long-range perspective, and willingness to change, relative to employees at their own

158

level, than managers in companies which have retained the Scanlon Plan. The differences are significant for eight of the ten traits and for a composite score based on responses to each of the ten traits.

The mean attitudes toward PDM for the managers in continuing and abandoned Scanlon Plan companies are presented in Table 10. As predicted, the managers in companies which have abandoned the Scanlon Plan have less favorable attitudes toward PDM than the managers in companies which have retained the Plan. Such differences are obtained for attitudes toward PDM as applied at the level of rank-and-file employees, at the level of the respondent's immediate subordinates, and at the respondent's own level. In addition, similar results are obtained for the general approval of PDM and for the perceived impact of participation on morale and performance. Although the data are not presented, the same pattern of results was obtained when the data were analyzed for each of the three participative policies separately.

Consistent with Lowin's model of change toward PDM and the case study literature on the Scanlon Plan, the results of this study indicated that management attitudes toward employees and toward PDM may mediate

TABLE 9

Means and t *Values for Confidence in Employees*

Trait	Continuing Scanlon Plan Firms[a]	Discontinued Scanlon Plan Firms[b]	t	p[c]
Judgment	2.27	2.56	−1.71	.05
Creativity	2.26	2.39	−1.34	n.s.
Responsibility	2.76	3.16	−1.77	.05
Dependability	2.07	2.62	2.33	.01
Pride in Performance	1.88	2.57	−3.00	.01
Alertness	2.17	2.57	−1.88	.01
Initiative	2.46	3.08	−3.05	.01
Self-Confidence	2.18	2.42	−1.03	n.s.
Long-range Perspective	2.94	3.62	−3.49	.01
Willingness to Change	2.29	3.19	−3.48	.01
Total	2.33	2.84	−3.23	.001

Note: $a_N = 130$; $b_N = 68$. [c]One-tailed test.

159

TABLE 10
Attitudes Toward Participative Decision Making

		As Applied at Level of Rank-and-File Employees			As Applied at Level of Immediate Subordinates			As Applied at Own Level		
		GA	*PIM*	PIP	GA	*PIM*	PIP	GA	*PIM*	PIP
Continuing	$\bar{X}$	3.99	4.31	3.91	4.25	4.41	4.20	4.35	4.41	4.23
Scanlon Plan	SD	.74	.59	.75	.58	.49	.59	.56	.53	.57
Firms	N	131	131	131	130	130	131	124	124	123
Discontinued	X	3.59	4.06	3.41	3.98	4.26	3.94	4.19	4.30	4.03
Scanlon Plan	SD	.82	.65	.72	.79	.49	.59	.68	.49	.62
Firms	n	71	71	70	71	70	70	67	67	67
t		3.55	2.78	4.52	2.68	1.98	2.92	1.73	1.34	2.16
p^{A}		.001	.01	.001	.01	.05	.01	.05	n.s.	.05

Note: Abbreviations: GA = general agreement; PIM = perceived impact on morale, PIP = perceived impact on performances. [a]One-tailed test.

the effects of efforts to implement the Scanlon Plan. Given the *post hoc* nature of this study's design, of course, caution must be exercised in interpreting these results; that is, it cannot be inferred from the results of this study that managerial attitudes caused the abandonment of the Scanlon Plan. It is also plausible, given the design of this study, that the abandonment of the Scanlon Plan, or more likely, factors associated with such abandonment, caused the observed differences in management attitudes.

In addition, several plausible interpretations of the specific causal sequence responsible for these results would be consistent with Lowin's model. First of all, for a variety of reasons, the attitudes toward PDM of the managers in the companies which abandoned the Scanlon Plan might not have been "unfrozen" to the extent necessary to allow PDM to develop. If this had happened, the Scanlon Plan would not have been effective in satisfying the needs of the employees or organizations involved and, consequently, would have been abandoned. Secondly, even if the attitudes of the managers involved were initially unfrozen, technological or individual difference variables not measured in this study could have prevented the complete development of PDM.[5] Under these circumstances, the Scanlon Plan would again fail to satisfy the needs of employees and of the organization, and this failure would result in both the abandonment of the Plan and less favorable management attitudes toward employees and PDM. Thirdly, even if management attitudes were initially unfrozen and PDM were able to develop, environmental[6] or individual difference[7] variables not measured in this study could have resulted in differential satisfaction of employee and organizational needs from PDM. Those companies in which PDM resulted in less satisfaction would then have been more likely to abandon the Scanlon Plan and to have managers with less favorable attitudes toward employees and toward participative decision making.

It seems likely that at least to some extent all the effects discussed above were operating in a mutually reinforcing manner to produce the observed relationship between management attitudes and retention of the Scanlon Plan. Further research, ideally employing longitudinal designs and the measurement of environmental, technological, and individual differences variables, is needed to assess the relative contributions of the effects discussed to this relationship. Certainly, simplistic hypotheses concerning the variables which affect the implementation of the Scanlon Plan are unlikely to do justice to the complexity of the relationships involved.

You and Your Job Survey

Lowin's model and the previous Scanlon Plan literature emphasize the importance of employee attitudes, as well as the attitudes of managers. However, as indicated in the preceding chapter, this literature contains little more than testimonials and anecdotes concerning the attitudes of employees about the Scanlon Plan. No previous studies have reported quantitative data concerning employee perceptions of or attitudes toward the Plan. In order to remedy this deficiency in our knowledge about the Scanlon Plan, the Scanlon Plan Associates and the Department of Psychology at Michigan State University jointly sponsored a major attitude survey. The project, which was initiated in 1968, was designed to provide a base line of data on the Scanlon Plan which could be supplemented with additional data over a period of time. The remaining studies to be reviewed in this chapter are all based on data from this project.

The primary research instrument used in this project was a questionnaire entitled "You and Your Job." This questionnaire included 275 items, covering a broad range of job-related attitudes, attitudes toward the Scanlon Plan, personal background variables, job needs or goals, and values. The questionnaire was distributed to all employees in twenty-seven geographically separated units of six manufacturing organizations in the Midwest. All organizations were active members of the Scanlon Plan Associates. The organizations ranged in size from approximately 150 to 3,500 employees. A total of 3,884 questionnaires were distributed, and 2,636 (65 percent) usable questionnaires were returned. More details concerning the data collection procedures, the organizations and individuals participating in the survey, and the methods of measurement and data analysis used in the studies reviewed in the remainder of this chapter are presented in the Appendix.

Employee Perceptions of the Scanlon Plan

Goodman, Wakeley, and Ruh analyzed data from the "You and Your Job" survey in order to assess employee perceptions and evaluations of the Scanlon Plan.[8] More specifically, employees were asked how they perceived and evaluated various aspects of the Scanlon Plan, such as the degree to which they were allowed to participate in decision making, the efficiency of the Scanlon Committees, and the overall utility of the Plan.

The results of this study indicated that employees saw various aspects of the Scanlon Plan differently and that they tended to order these differences consistently. The pattern of responses across the items seemed to indicate a trichotomy on the general dimensions of favorableness toward the Scanlon Plan. There are those items which reflect *very positive* attitudes, those which reflect *positive* attitudes, and those items which reflect *slightly negative* attitudes.

VERY POSITIVE ASPECTS

Two items reflect *very positive* attitudes toward the Scanlon Plan and indicate that the majority of employees see that:

1. The Scanlon Plan has helped this company's financial position.
2. The Scanlon Plan encourages hard work.

The item with the most positive response was the first one. This result seems to indicate that the employees see the plan as having real, practical utility. People working within the Plan see it as having payoffs for the organization. Such payoffs, of course, should also result in greater security for those who are employed by the organization.

A further analysis on this item tested whether the favorable response to the item was an artifact of employees simply saying the Plan has helped the company's financial position because in theory it should. The assumption was made that employees at higher levels within a company have more complete and accurate data on the financial position of the company. The total sample was divided into three groups: managers, first-line supervisors, and rank-and-file employees. Responses among the three groups were then compared. The results of this comparison indicated a definite linear pattern: managers responded more favorably than supervisors, who in turn responded more favorably than rank-and-file employees. It appears that those who can most accurately judge the value of the Plan were most favorably impressed with the Plan.

Returning to the total sample, it appears the employees "agree" that "the Scanlon Plan encourages hard work." This finding adds credence to the basic idea of participative decision making. Frequently, it is thought that if employees are allowed to decide what to do and how to do it, they will probably decide not to do it at all. However, it appears, at least as the employees see it, that the success of the Plan is, in part, due to hard work. The Scanlon Plan is not a give-away program, but a system which defines a different set of roles for the participants, a unique way of assessing organizational efficiency, and a means by which employees can be compensated for improvements in organizational efficiency. The difference is that employees are now an integral part of the organization.

POSITIVE ASPECTS

Items 3 to 8 reflect *positive attitudes* toward the Scanlon Plan and indicate that employees see that:

3. . . . the Scanlon Plan is more than merely a nice idea.
4. . . . the Scanlon Plan increases their knowledge about the company.
5. . . . the Scanlon Plan increases their trust and confidence in management.
6. . . . the Scanlon Plan helps them to do their jobs better.
7. . . . the Scanlon Committees improve company efficiency.
8. . . . it is worthwhile to offer suggestions to the Scanlon Committees.

Again, the implications are that the employees see the Plan as having real utility as an organizational system. Similarly, they see specific mechanisms of the Plan—that is, suggestions and committees—as functioning fairly well in accomplishing the goal of organizational efficiency.

Three items indicate that employees have reservations about the implementation of the Scanlon Plan in their organizations. Specifically, employees are slightly negative about:

9. . . . the extent to which the Plan allows them to really influence decisions which affect their jobs.
10. . . . the extent to which the Plan provides them with an opportunity to learn more about their jobs.
11. . . . the fact that the Plan may be a way for management to get more out of the workers.

The message which seems to be coming through from these data is that employees are to some extent questioning the underlying intent of the Plan as they see it in operation. A question arises as to whether or not the basic philosophy of the Scanlon Plan has, in fact, been put into operation within the organizations surveyed. From the results obtained, this particular question cannot be completely answered, but the evidence is sufficient to suspect that the answer would be "not completely." It appears that "participation" within the companies surveyed is defined largely as, "increased information" and is typified, for example, in the favorable responses of employees to the item "the Scanlon Plan helps me learn more about the whole company." Granted, increased information is essential within a participative system, but it is not sufficient. True participation, that which the Scanlon Plan advocates, requires a secondary element, influence. Within the present group it appears that a less than optimal amount of the second element is present in regard to employee influence on decisions which affect their jobs.

A frequent retort to the above kind of results is, "Well that's okay because employees really don't want to make decisions anyway. They would rather just do what they are told and not be involved any more than they have to." The Scanlon philosophy, on the other hand, contends that most employees do want to participate and, if given the opportunity, will participate in the decision-making process. Support for this latter statement was drawn from the survey in the employee's responses to another item which asked "Would you like to be a representative on a Production Committee?" Nearly forty percent of the employees answered yes. Given the fact that being a member of a committee means more work, more responsibility, and more hours (usually without compensation), the forty percent positive response is support for the idea that people do want to participate. Unfortunately, the percentage of employees who want to participate on a less formal basis—that is, in their immediate work group—cannot be identified. However, there is reason to suspect that it would probably be considerably higher than the percentage who wish to participate at the total system level.

SUMMARY

Overall, the results of this study indicated that the Plan does have practical utility as an organizational system and the mechanics of the Plan (that is, suggestions and committees) are functioning fairly well. However, the intent of the Plan appears to be less than fully realized as evidenced by the fact that the employees do not see themselves participating within the system to the extent implied by the theory of the Scanlon Plan. The shortcomings found in the present study appear to reflect faulty implementation rather than inherent flaws in the principles and assumptions upon which the Scanlon Plan is based.

The Scanlon Plan, PDM, and Job Attitudes

Theoretical literature on the Scanlon Plan, previous chapters in this book, and Lowin's model all share the view that it is changes in the underlying dimensions of the Scanlon Plan, such as PDM, rather than the adoption of the Plan's formal, structural "mechanics," that is, the committee and bonus systems, which contribute to the "desirable" effects that have reportedly resulted from installations of the Scanlon Plan. This hypothesis certainly seems plausible and is consistent with the results of several case studies. On the other hand, Gray concluded that the Scanlon Plan failed in the case he studied for reasons unrelated to management or supervisory style.[9] In addition, as indicated in the previous chapter, no studies had been designed specifically to investigate the effect of PDM on the implementation of the Scanlon Plan.

A study by Patchen, while not directly focused on the Scanlon Plan, is relevant in this connection.[10] Patchen investigated the impact of the "cooperative program" at the Tennessee Valley Authority (TVA) on employee job attitudes. The TVA cooperative program is similar to the Scanlon Plan in philosophy and in formal structure. The main difference between the two systems is that the TVA program does not include a bonus system. Patchen's results could be interpreted as generally consistent with the theoretical positions of both Lowin and the Scanlon Plan literature. That is, Patchen's results did provide some indication that employee attitudes toward a formal participation system and perceptions of the extent to which the system served as an "active channel for participation in work decisions" were positively related to job attitudes.

More specifically, Patchen's results indicated that the "perceived vigor" of the TVA program (employee perceptions of the interest in the program, information received about the program and effectiveness of the program) and the extent to which the program was seen as an active channel for participation were positively related to employee identification with the organization and acceptance of change. The vigor of the program and participation through the program, on the other hand, were not significantly related to job motivation or interest in innovation. In addition, the results indicated that participation through the cooperative program was most strongly related to identification with the organization for those work groups in which there was also a high degree of influence in the immediate job situation.

Patchen's data also indicated that the relationship between PDM and identification with the organization was moderated somewhat by occupational status. Several measures of influence and participation in the immediate job situation were more strongly related to identification with the organization for professional engineers than for skilled workers. The correlations between participation through the cooperative program and identification with the organization, however, were the same for both types of employees.

There is some indication in the literature, then, that formalized systems designed to facilitate large-scale, organization-wide increases in PDM, such as the Scanlon Plan, may contribute to "favorable" employee job attitudes and that variations in the extent to which such systems are seen as providing viable channels for PDM may be related to their effectiveness. In addition, there is some indication that the impact of such systems on job attitudes may be conditioned by the extent of participation in the immediate job situation and by occupational status.

THE PROBLEM

Ruh, Johnson, and Scontrino, therefore, designed a study to investigate more thoroughly the relationships among those variables with respect to the Scanlon Plan PDM system.[11] More specifically, the study was designed to explore the following hypotheses:

1. There are systematic differences among organizational units employing the Scanlon Plan in the extent to which the Plan is seen as an effective channel for PDM.
2. Such variations in the extent to which the Scanlon Plan is seen as an effective channel for PDM are positively related to employee job attitudes.
3. There is an interaction between PDM through the Scanlon Plan and PDM in the immediate job situation, such that the relationships between PDM through the Scanlon Plan and job attitudes are more positive when there is a high degree of PDM in the immediate job situation than when there is a low degree of such PDM.
4. The relationships between PDM through the Scanlon Plan and job attitudes are more positive for individuals in management positions than for rank-and-file employees.

RESULTS AND DISCUSSION

The results of this study indicated that there were significant differences between organizational units operating under the Scanlon Plan in the extent to which the Plan was seen as providing an effective vehicle for participation in decision making (F = 14.77; p < .001). The unit means on this variable ranged from 2.78 to 3.65, with a total sample mean of 3.19. In addition, the results, summarized in Table 11, indicated that such perceptions of the Scanlon Plan were positively related to job involvement, motivation, and identification with the organization. These results are consistent with Lowin's theoretical model of PDM change, previous case histories of the Scanlon Plan, and the results of Patchen's investigation of TVA's cooperative program, all of which predict that the Scanlon Plan should contribute to favorable employee attitudes to the extent to which it provides opportunities for participation in decision making. Participation in the immediate job situation was also positively related to job attitudes.

Given the correlational nature of this study's design, however, caution should be exercised in interpreting the results. For example, it could be plausibly argued that rather than variations in the extent to which the Scanlon Plan provides opportunities for participation influencing job attitudes as suggested above, job attitudes may influence perceptions of the Scanlon Plan. That is, although it seems unlikely that the Scanlon Plan would contribute to job involvement, motivation, and identification with the organization without providing opportunities for participation in decision making, it also seems plausible that highly involved, motivated, and identified employees may be more likely to perceive the Scanlon Plan as an

167

TABLE 11

Correlations of Participation Through the Scanlon Plan and in the
Immediate Job Situation with Job Attitudes

Job Attitudes	Participation Through the Scanlon Plan			Participation in the Immediate Job Situation		
	Units[a]	Work groups[b]	Individuals[c]	Units	Work groups	Individual
Job involve- ment	.88	.51	.43	.90	.70	.51
Motivation	.56	.34	.30	.66	.49	.37
Identification	.73	.48	.40	.77	.64	.46

Note: All correlations are significant at p $< .05$. $a_N = 15$; $b_N = 180$; $c_N = 2488$

effective vehicle for participation than employees with less positive attitudes. In addition, supervisors may well be more responsive to the ideas and
inputs of subordinates with more favorable attitudes. Very likely all these
processes are operating in a mutually reinforcing manner. Additional research employing longitudinal designs is needed to assess the relative contributions of these different effects to the observed correlations between perceived participation through the Scanlon Plan and employee attitudes
toward the job.

Contrary to Patchen's results in his TVA study, the relationships between
participation through the Scanlon Plan and job attitudes were not consistently moderated by participation in the immediate job situation or occupational status. Similarly, the correlations between participation in the immediate job situation and job attitudes were not consistently moderated by
occupational status. These results are summarized in Table 12.

The failure of participation in the immediate job situation to moderate
the relationships between participation through the Scanlon Plan and job
attitudes in the present study could have been due to the relatively high
correlation (.52 for individuals and .67 for work groups) between the two
forms of participation for this sample. On the other hand, there does not
seem to be any particularly compelling reason, other than Patchen's results,
to expect participation through the Scanlon Plan and participation in the
immediate job situation to relate to job attitudes in an interactive rather
than additive and compensatory manner.

Several factors could account for the inconsistency between the results

TABLE 12
Correlations Between Participation Through the Scanlon Plan and Job
Attitudes as a Function of Participation in the Immediate Job Situation
Occupational Status

Job Attitudes	Participation in the Immediate Job Situation			Occupational Status	
	Low	Medium	High	Rank and File	Management
Job involvement	.33	.22	.27	.38	.38
Motivation	.15	.16	.16	.27	.33
Identification	.28	.25	.27	.36	.39
N	854	870	881	2065	298

Note: All correlations are for the individual level of analysis. No correlations
are significantly different between high and low participation in the immediate
job situation or management and rank- and file- subgroups.

of this study and Patchen's results with respect to the moderating effects
of occupational status on the relationships of participation through the
Scanlon Plan and in the immediate job situation with job attitudes. First of
all, Patchen's results indicated that only the relationships between participation in the immediate job situation and identification with the organization were significantly different for employees of different occupational
status. The correlations between participation through the cooperative program and identification with the organization were the same for both types
of employees. The relatively high correlation between participation through
the Scanlon Plan and participation in immediate job situation obtained in
the present study obviously reduced the opportunity for such differential
results. In addition, the occupational groups involved in the present study
were different from those studied by Patchen. In the present study, the
correlations between participation and job attitudes for rank-and-file employees were compared with the correlations between these variables for
individuals occupying management positions, whereas Patchen compared
professional engineers and skilled blue-collar workers. It is difficult to assess
the effects of this difference, since both "measures" are relatively gross
classifications which cut across several individual difference and situational
variables. Future research should, therefore, focus on more precisely specified individual difference and situational variables as possible moderators

of the relationships between participation in decision making and employee responses to the job.

Individual Differences and the Scanlon Plan

It is widely recognized that no two people are alike and that differences among people can reasonably be expected to affect their responses to the job situation. In general, however, organizational psychologists and others interested in improving organizations by making them more compatible with human needs have tended to ignore the effects of individual differences on responses to job and organizational characteristics.

For example, the previous Scanlon Plan literature contains little, if any, reference to possible differences among people in their reactions to the Scanlon Plan in general or to specific aspects of the Plan, such as PDM. Lowin's model, on the other hand, directs our attention to the systematic investigation of such differences.

In addition, as indicated in the preceding chapter, there is some evidence in the literature that individuals with different backgrounds, needs, and values may respond differently to PDM, a key element of the Scanlon Plan. Therefore, several studies jointly sponsored by the Scanlon Plan Associates and Michigan State University in recent years have been devoted to the investigation of the possible effects of individual differences in personal background, values, and needs on employee responses to the job in general and to job and organizational characteristics, such as PDM, in particular.

EDUCATION, EGO NEED GRATIFICATION, AND JOB ATTITUDES

The Problem. Ruh, Wakeley, and Morrison[12] investigated several hypotheses derived from an integration of the theoretical positions of those who advocate participative management and job enrichment[13] and the speculations of Schein.[14] In essence, the former theorists contend that ego need gratification (ENG) is positively related to favorable responses to the job for everyone, or at least for most individuals working in modern industrial organizations. Schein, on the other hand, hypothesized that ENG is more likely to be positively related to employee responses to the job for more educated individuals than for individuals with less education. Schein did not specify the nature of the relationship between ENG and employee responses to be expected for individuals with less education. For the purpose of this study, therefore, it was hypothesized that ENG is positively related to

170

employee responses at all levels of education, but that this relationship is stronger for more educated individuals than for individuals with less education. In addition, this study investigated hypotheses derived from the idea that desires for ENG, or the importance placed on ENG, is an intervening variable "through which" education interacts with ENG.

More formally, this study was designed to test the following hypotheses:

1. The extent of ENG provided by the job is positively related to employee job attitudes.
2. Education moderates the relationships between ENG and job attitudes, such that the relationships between ENG and job attitudes are more positive for more educated individuals than for those individuals with less education.
3. Education is positively related to the importance of ENG (IENG).
4. IENG moderates the relationships between ENG and job attitudes, such that ENG is more positively related to job attitudes for those individuals for whom such gratification is more important than for those individuals for whom such gratification is less important.

RESULTS AND DISCUSSION

The results of this study are summarized in Tables 13 and 14.

In general, the results confirmed both the prediction of positive relationships between ENG and job attitudes, which was derived from the participative management theoretical position, and the prediction of an interaction between education and ENG, which was derived from the theoretical speculations of Schein. The hypothesized role of IENG as an intervening variable "through which" education interacts with ENG was not supported. IENG was positively related to education. However, the relationship was very slight, and no support was found for the hypothesized interaction between IENG and ENG. The reasons for these ambiguous results are not at all clear, but the validity of the measurement of the IENG could certainly be questioned.

The results of the present study were generally consistent with the theoretical positions of both the participative management theorists and those authors who stress the important of a "complex man" perspective on the interaction between the individual and the organization. It is especially interesting that the results were consistent with both of these theoretical positions in light of the rather polemic attacks of some of the advocates of the "complex man" position[15] on the position of the participative manage-

171

TABLE 13
Correlations Between ENG and Job Attitudes as a Function of Education

Education	N	ENG Measure					
		HL			PENG		
		INV	MOT	IDEN	INV	MOT	IDEN
High	457	.50	.25	.47	.75	.55	.67
Medium	983	.30	.16	.24	.65	.45	.46
Low	780	.22	.12	.17	.57	.43	.43
Total	2220	.35	.17	.28	.66	.47	.52

Note: INV = job involvement; MOT = intrinsic motivation; IDEN = identification. All correlations are significant at $p < .01$.

TABLE 14
Correlations Between ENG and Job Attitudes as a Function of IENG

Education	N	ENG Measure					
		HL			PENG		
		INV	MOT	IDEN	INV	MOT	IDEN
High	721	.34	.14	.28	.68	.48	.53
Medium	728	.34	.16	.31	.64	.44	.50
Low	771	.36	.18	.25	.63	.48	.51

ment theorists. Essentially, the results of the present study indicated that, while the basic proposition of the participative management theorists concerning the relationships between ENG and employee responses to the job is probably tenable, more variance in employee responses to the job could be accounted for if that proposition were refined to include interactions between individual differences and the extent of ENG provided by the job.

JOB INVOLVEMENT, PDM, AND PERSONAL BACKGROUND

The Problem. In a similar study, Siegel and Ruh investigated the relationships between job involvement (JI) and PDM, personal background variables, and job behavior.[16] Job involvement was defined as the extent to which the individual identifies with his work or the importance of work to his self-image.

The background variables chosen for study were level of education and community size. As indicated earlier in this chapter, Schein suggested that while opportunities for the fulfillment of higher order needs may contribute to favorable employee responses to the job for highly educated individuals, this relationship may not hold for less well-educated employees. Similarly, there is some evidence that job attitudes may be positively related to opportunity for higher order need fulfillment for workers with rural or small town backgrounds but not for urban workers.[17] Therefore, it was, hypothesized that JI would be positively related to education and negatively related to community size, and that the relationship between JI and PDM would be more positive for more highly educated individuals and for individuals from smaller communities than for individuals with less education and more urban backgrounds.

RESULTS AND DISCUSSION

The total sample correlations of JI with PDM, performance, absenteeism, turnover, education, and community size are presented in Table 15.

The correlational nature of these data precludes unambiguous cause-and-effect inferences. On the whole, however, these results are consistent with the hypothesis that PDM is a determinant of job attitudes and motivation. PDM, as measured in the present study, was positively related to JI for the total sample and within each of the education and community size subgroups. These results are also consistent with previous research which has found JI to be positively related to job characteristics similar to PDM.[18]

On the other hand, the results of the present study are generally inconsistent with Lodahl and Kejner's original hypothesis that JI is a value orientation which is learned early in the socialization process and is relatively unaffected by situational organizational variables.[19] Of the two background variables investigated in the present study, only community size was signifi-

TABLE 15
Total Sample Correlations of JI with PDM Job Behaviors and Personal Background Variables

	Performance	Absenteeism	Turnover	Education	PDM	Community Size
Correlation with JI	.03	.02	−.17*	.00	.51*	.21*
N	398	238	1662	2530	2628	2572

*p < .01

173

cantly correlated with JI. In addition, the direction of the relationship between JI and community size was opposite from that indicated by previous research and theory.[20] That is, the results of this study indicated that JI was positively related to community size.

In general, a "complex man" theoretical position (Schein, 1971), which emphasizes interactions between individual differences and job and organizational characteristics, seems to account for more variance in employee responses to the job than an exclusive concentration on either class of variables. In the present study, therefore, rather than looking to PDM or personal background as *the* determinant of JI, it was hypothesized that both PDM and personal background variables would be related to JI and that personal background would moderate the relationship between PDM and JI. Consistent with this general hypothesis, the relationship between JI and PDM was moderated by education and community size. These results are summarized in Table 16.

As expected, the correlation between PDM and JI was significantly more positive for those individuals in the high education subgroup than for those individuals in the low education subgroup. These results are consistent with Schein's suggestion that education may influence desires for and expectations about higher order need fulfillment on the job in such a manner as to result in differential relationships between job and organizational characteristics and employee responses to the job for different education subgroups. Unexpectedly, the correlation between JI and PDM was least positive for the medium education subgroup. The reason for this finding is not at all

TABLE 16
Correlation Between JI and PDM as a Function of Education and Community Size

	Education			Community Size		
	High	Medium	Low	High	Medium	Low
Correlation between JI and PDM	.62	.42	.51	.55	.48	.43
N	488	919	1123	857	858	856

Note: All correlations are significant at p < .01. The differences between the correlation for the high and low subgroups are significant at p < .01 for both education and community size.

174

clear. It would seem, however, that future research on the moderating effects of personal background variables should examine the full range of such variables, as opposed to comparing only extreme groups, if we are to fully understand the complexity of the relationships involved.

Consistent with the finding that community size was related to JI in the direction opposite to that predicted by previous theory and research, community size moderated the relationship between PDM and JI in the direction opposite from that hypothesized. That is, the correlation between PDM and JI was more positive for the more urban individuals than for the less urban individuals. Hulin and Blood presented a model of the relationships among individual differences, job characteristics, and employee responses to the job which would predict the opposite relationship between community size and the correlation between PDM and JI.[21] According to Hulin and Blood's model, urbanization leads to "alienation from middle class work norms." Individuals who are thus alienated are said to not expect or desire higher order need fulfillment from their jobs and to respond "negatively" to job characteristics similar to PDM.

The results of two previous investigations of the moderating effects of community characteristics on the relationships between job characteristics and employee responses to the job[22] were cited by Hulin and Blood as supporting their model. The specific variables, measurement procedures, and subject samples involved in the Blood and Hulin and Turner and Lawrence studies all differed from those of the present study. Therefore, it is impossible to determine the reasons for the conflicting results obtained with any degree of certainty. It should be noted, however, that in both of the previous studies, the urbanization of the plant sites involved was used to moderate the relationships between job characteristics and employee responses. Neither study directly investigated the effects of the size of community in which the employees had been raised, currently live, or preferred to live, as was done in the present study. In addition, in both studies the final data analyses, which yielded the results cited by Hulin and Blood as supporting their model, were actually only subsets of the total set of analyses performed on the same data and were not performed until the initial analyses failed to produce significant results. Blood and Hulin, for example, found no consistent support for their hypotheses in their original sample, which included both white- and blue-collar employees, and even when they restricted their analysis to blue-collar workers, only four out of eighty-four correlations were significant at the .01 level of confidence. It

175

would seem, therefore, that more research is needed to clarify the effects of community variables on the relationships between job characteristics and employee responses. Longitudinal studies that include direct measures of individual value orientations in addition to community characteristics and personal background would be particularly appropriate.

The results of the present study did not indicate that JI was consistently or strongly related to job behaviors. Consistent with the results of Farris,[23] the correlation between JI and turnover was significant and negative. The amount of variance accounted for by this relationship (slightly less than three percent), on the other hand, indicates that JI may not have a great deal of practical utility as a prediction of turnover. In addition, JI was not significantly related to absenteeism or performance. Problems involved with the measurement of these variables, however, preclude unambiguous interpretations of these results.

Job performance was measured by averaging weekly productivity, expressed as a percentage of engineered standards, over a twenty-week period beginning seventeen months subsequent to the collection of questionnaire data. Several potential problems are associated with this measure. First of all, the length of the time interval between the collection of the JI and performance data may have attenuated the relationship between these variables. The potential for such attenuation was increased by the fact that the organization studied underwent several changes, including major changes in its compensation and work measurement systems, during this time interval. Secondly, since most of the jobs involved were of a production line nature, the employees exercised less than complete control over their individual productivity rate. Finally, a plausible case can be made for the argument that the quality of job performance may be more likely be related to attitudinal variables such as JI than to the quantity of job performance.[24] The measure of performance used in the present study, however, was based almost exclusively on the quantity of performance.

Absenteeism was measured by the proportion of hours absent to total hours worked for the same twenty-week period for which performance data were collected. The collection of the JI and absenteeism data were therefore separated by the same time lag and intervening events that separated the collection of JI and performance data. In addition, total hours absent is not likely to be very sensitive to employee attitudes and motivation in that this measure may be heavily influenced by lengthy periods of absence due to accidents or illness.

176

Further research is obviously needed before firm conclusions concerning the relationships between JI and performance, absenteeism, and turnover can be drawn. Studies in which measures of the quality of job performance, absence frequency, and shorter time intervals between the collection of JI and job behavior data are employed would be particularly fruitful.

PDM, VALUES, AND JOB ATTITUDES

The Problem. Finally, White, Ruh, and Morrison investigated the moderating effects of individual values on the relationships between PDM and attitudes toward the job.[25] On the basis of theoretical analyses of Hulin and Blood, Patchen, Strauss, and Vroom, it was hypothesized that the following values would moderate the relationships between participation in decision making and job attitudes: *a sense of accomplishment, ambitious, capable, equality, freedom, imaginative, independent, responsible, self-control,* and *participation.* More specifically, it was hypothesized that the relationships between participation in decision making and job involvement, motivation, and identification with the organization are more positive for individuals who attach high importance to these values than for individuals who attach low importance to these values.

RESULTS AND DISCUSSION

The correlations of participation in decision making with job involvement, motivation, and identification with the organization for the worker, management, and total samples are presented in Table 17. These correlations are all positive and statistically significant (p < .01).

Table 18 presents the correlation of participation in decision making with job attitudes within the high, medium, and low value subgroups for the rank-and-file workers. Table 19 presents these correlations for the management sample. Inspection of these data reveals no support for the hypothesized moderating effects. All 180 of the correlations presented in Tables 18 and 19 are positive, and the great majority (166) are greater than .30. Only fourteen of the sixty rankings of correlations conformed to the predicted rankings. That is, the correlations of participation in decision making with job attitudes decreased monotonically from the high to the low value subgroups in only fourteen instances. The chance expectation is that ten of the rankings would conform to the hypothesis. Ten of the rankings were in the direction opposite to that predicted, and the remainder were curvilinear.

177

TABLE 17
Correlations Between Participation in Decision Making and Job Attitudes

Attitude	Sample		
	Total	Workers	Managers
Involvement	.53	.44	.53
	(2750)	(2183)	(384)
Motivation	.38	.34	.39
	(2750)	(2183)	(384)
Identification	.47	.40	.39
	(2730)	(2168)	(383)

Note: The numbers in parentheses indicate the number of observations on which the correlations are based. All correlations are significant at $p < .01$.

TABLE 18

Correlations Between Participation in Decision Making and Job Attitudes for the Value Subgroups of Workers

Value	Value Group			Rank Order of Correlations Monotonic?	If Monotonic in Predicted Direction?	If in Predicted Direction, Similar Finding for Managers?
	Hi	Med	Low			
Accomplishment						
Involvement	.45	.46	.41	No		
Motivation	.32	.32	.33	No		
Identification	.43	.41	.36	Yes		
Equality						
Involvement	.41	.44	.49	Yes	No	
Motivation	.27	.33	.39	Yes	No	
Identification	.39	.38	.43	No		
Freedom						
Involvement	.40	.50	.43	No		
Motivation	.26	.37	.34	No		
Identification	.38	.43	.34	No		
Ambitious						
Involvement	.43	.45	.43	No		
Motivation	.27	.36	.34	No		
Identification	.40	.42	.38	No		
Capable						
Involvement	.48	.42	.42	Yes	Yes	No
Motivation	.36	.33	.30	Yes	Yes	Yes
Identification	.43	.39	.39	No		

Value	Hi	Med	Low	Monotonic?	In Predicted Direction?	Similar Finding for Workers?
Imaginative						
Involvement	.51	.46	.34	Yes	Yes	No
Motivation	.41	.32	.25	Yes	Yes	No
Identification	.44	.40	.35	Yes	Yes	No
Independent						
Involvement	.41	.48	.44	No		
Motivation	.33	.33	.33	No		
Identification	.38	.43	.40	No		
Responsible						
Involvement	.45	.42	.46	No		
Motivation	.29	.34	.35	Yes	No	
Identification	.39	.38	.44	No		
Self-Control						
Involvement	.46	.44	.43	Yes	Yes	No
Motivation	.32	.32	.34	No		
Identification	.39	.41	.41	No		
Participation						
Involvement	.44	.46	.42	No		
Motivation	.35	.38	.27	No		
Identification	.41	.45	.33	No		

Note: Sample size ranged from 483 to 838. Median N = 603.

TABLE 19

Correlations Between Participation in Decision Making and Job Attitudes for the Value Subgroups of Workers

Value	Value Group			Rank Order of Correlations Monotonic?	If Monotonic in Predicted Direction?	If in Predicted Direction, Similar Finding for Workers?
	Hi	Med	Low			
Accomplishment						
Involvement	.45	.55	.50	No		
Motivation	.41	.33	.36	No		
Identification	.25	.45	.50	Yes	No	
Equality						
Involvement	.63	.48	.45	Yes	Yes	No
Motivation	.22	.40	.45	Yes	No	
Identification	.49	.42	.34	Yes	Yes	No
Freedom						
Involvement	.55	.50	.49	Yes	Yes	No
Motivation	.40	.47	.24	No		
Identification	.44	.38	.40	No		

179

Ambitious							
Involvement	.59	.57	.43	Yes	Yes	No
Motivation	.46	.54	.11	No		
Identification	.38	.42	.44	Yes	No	
Capable							
Involvement	.61	.41	.51	No		
Motivation	.48	.31	.30	Yes	Yes	Yes
Identification	.32	.37	.52	Yes	No	
Imaginative							
Involvement	.44	.57	.54	No		
Motivation	.39	.45	.31	No		
Identification	.34	.40	.47	Yes	No	
Independent							
Involvement	.46	.57	.57	No		
Motivation	.40	.46	.30	No		
Identification	.41	.37	.47	No		
Responsible							
Involvement	.43	.54	.62	Yes	No	
Motivation	.33	.38	.41	Yes	No	
Identification	.42	.26	.52	No		
Self-Control							
Involvement	.53	.48	.58	No		
Motivation	.20	.48	.45	No		
Identification	.49	.41	.33	Yes	Yes	No
Participation							
Involvement	.55	.53	.51	Yes	Yes	No
Motivation	.39	.42	.33	No		
Identification	.42	.32	.50	No		

Note: Sample size ranged from 97 to 149. Median N = 120.

agement samples. The fourteen rankings which were in the predicted direction were divided equally between the worker and management samples, and only one ranking (the correlations between participation and identification for employees subgrouped on the value *capable*) was in the predicted direction for both samples. Furthermore, the different values provided little differential support for the hypothesis. The rank order of correlations was in the predicted direction for all three attitudes for only one value *(imaginative)*, and this result held only for the worker sample. Five of the eight values for which rankings in the predicted direction were obtained also yielded rankings in the opposite direction. Finally, there were no systematic values for which rankings in the predicted direction were obtained also yielded rankings in the opposite direction. Finally, there were no systematic differences in the support provided for the hypothesis by the three different job attitudes.

The results of this study were consistent with the participative management proposition concerning the effects of participation in decision making on attitudes toward the job. Participation in decision making, as measured in this study, was consistently related positively to job involvement, motivation, and identification with the organization. Given the correlational nature of this study's design and the self-report nature of the measures employed, of course, caution must be exercised in interpreting these results. As indicated earlier in this chapter, it could be plausibly argued that rather than variations in the extent of participation in decision making influencing job attitudes as suggested by the participative management theorists, job attitudes may influence participation in decision making, particularly as measured by self-reports. Several factors could contribute to such a causal sequence. First of all, it is conceivable that highly involved, motivated, and identified employees may be more likely to perceive or report a higher degree of participation than employees with less favorable job attitudes, independent of any objective differences in participation. Such an effect could result from the operation of "response sets"[26] or from the fact that the participation and job attitudes measures were to some extent both tapping "general job satisfaction." In addition, supervisors may well be more responsive to the ideas and suggestions of subordinates with more favorable job attitudes.[27] Very likely, all these processes are operating in a mutually reinforcing manner. Additional research employing longitudinal designs and objective as well as self-report measures of participation is needed to assess the relative contributions of these different effects to the observed correlations between participation and job attitudes.

Contrary to expectations, values did not consistently moderate the relationships between participation and job attitudes. Several methodological problems could have contributed to these "negative" results. First of all, any common method variance in the measures of job attitudes and participation would inflate the correlations between these variables and could reduce the opportunity for moderating effects. Secondly, the reliability of the value data is somewhat suspect. The ranking of two sets of eighteen socially desirable values, particularly at the end of a lengthy questionnaire,

181

is not an easy task, nor one that would be enthusiastically welcomed. Inspection of these data indicated that, in fact, many subjects did not follow the instructions. Thirdly, the Value Survey is an ipsative measure, while the theoretical rationale for the hypothesized moderating effects of values on the relationships between participation and job attitudes implies normative measurement. It is conceivable, for example, that on an absolute scale some of the subjects in the "low" accomplishment group could actually attach more importance to accomplishment than some of the subjects in the "high" accomplishment group.

It is, of course, impossible to determine to what extent the lack of hypothesized results should be attributed to such measurement problems. It should be pointed out, however, that the importance of participation, which was not difficult to respond to, was located toward the beginning of the questionnaire, and was not ipsative, provided no more support for the hypothesized moderating effects than did the Rokeach values.

In addition to these measurement problems, characteristics of the sample of organizations and employees involved in the present study may have contributed to the lack of moderating effects. All plants were located in the Midwest, and only two plants were located in large industrialized cities. This factor could have restricted the range of employee values, such that individuals who were extremely "alienated from middle class norms" may have been excluded from the sample. It should be noted in this connection, however, that the median rankings of the Rokeach values in the present sample correlated .90 (terminal values) and .93 (instrumental values) with the median rankings obtained in a white national probability sample.[28]

There is, of course, one other possible interpretation for the lack of moderating effects. That is, the participative management theorists may be correct in de-emphasizing the importance of individual differences on the relationships between job characteristics and employee responses. It is difficult to imagine that individual differences in general and values in particular have no systematic effects on employee responses to participation in decision making. However, it may be that such effects are not as great as some of the critics of the participative management position would have us believe.[29] Clearly, more research is needed before it can be concluded that values exert any systematic influence on the relationship between participation in decision making and attitudes toward the job.

Summary—Implications for Practice and Future Research

In this chapter we have seen concrete illustrations of the type of research which must be conducted if the implementation of the Scanlon Plan in the future is to benefit from increased social science knowledge. These studies also illustrate that the Scanlon Plan provides an excellent entree for research, as well as for organization development.

The results of the research reviewed in this chapter are, of course, far from unambiguous. The surface of scientific knowledge about the Scanlon Plan has really just been scratched. However, the results of these studies do point in certain directions. A consistent theme running throughout the results of all the studies is the central role of PDM in the implementation of the Scanlon Plan. In every instance in which PDM was correlated with job attitudes, a positive, statistically significant, and relatively large correlation was obtained. Positive correlations were obtained even for those subgroups of employees who, according to previous theory and research, should not be particularly eager to participate in decision making. These results, coupled with the findings that management attitudes toward PDM and toward employees are correlated with retention of the Scanlon Plan[30], clearly indicate that the emphasis placed on PDM in the previous chapters of this book and in the previous literature on the Scanlon Plan is not misplaced.

The practical significance of these results for the implementation of the Scanlon Plan is increased by the finding that employees perceive the Scanlon Plan as providing less than optimal opportunities for participation in decision making. The implications of these results for organization development in general and for the implementation of the Scanlon Plan in particular seem clear: ways must be found and implemented to increase opportunities for employees to influence decisions which affect their jobs.

These results also have implications for future research needs. Consistent with the prescriptions offered in the preceding chapter, the results of the research reviewed in this chapter indicate that future research should emphasize the quantitative investigation of variables which are likely to mediate the effectiveness of the PDM process. Particular attention should be devoted to the study of potential obstacles to the implementation of PDM and to the effectiveness of ways to overcome such obstacles. Such a research emphasis obviously would be quite complementary to the development program suggested above. This complementariness provides support for the basic premise of these chapters: in human and organizational affairs, just as in the realm of engineering and physics, progress in practical application requires progress in knowledge from scientific research.

NOTES TO CHAPTER 7

1. Lowin, 1968.
2. Gray, 1971.
3. Ruh, Wallace, and Frost, 1972.
4. Miles, 1965.
5. Strauss, 1963.
6. Lawrence and Lorsch, 1967.
7. Hulin and Blood, 1968.
8. Goodman, Wakeley, and Ruh, 1972.
9. Gray, 1971.
10. Patchen, 1965.
11. Ruh, Johnson, and Scontrino, 1972.
12. Ruh, Wakeley, and Morrison, 1972.
13. Argyris, 1964; Herzberg, 1966; Likert, 1961; McGregor, 1960.
14. Schein, 1971.
15. Hulin and Blood, 1968; MacKinney et al., 1962; Strauss, 1963.
16. Siegel and Ruh, 1972.
17. Blood and Hulin, 1967; Hulin and Blood, 1968; Turner and Lawrence, 1965.
18. Lawler and Hall, 1970; Maurer, 1967; Patchen, 1965.
19. Lodahl and Kejner, 1965.
20. Hulin and Blood, 1968; Turner and Lawrence, 1965.
21. Hulin and Blood, 1968.
22. Blood and Hulin, 1967; Turner and Lawrence, 1965.
23. Farris, 1971.
24. Lawler, 1970.
25. White, Ruh, and Morrison, 1972.
26. Guilford, 1954.
27. Farris, 1969; Farris and Lim, 1969; Lowin and Craig, 1968.
28. Rokeach and Parker, 1970.
29. Hulin and Blood, 1968; MacKinney et al., 1962, Strauss, 1963.
30. Ruh, Wallace, and Frost, 1972.

APPENDIX

Methodological Details

YOU AND YOUR JOB SURVEY

Data Collection. The data were collected under the auspices of the Scanlon Plan Associates and Michigan State University. Research teams of several graduate students and faculty visited each organization in order to explain the purpose and nature of the research and to distribute the questionnaires. The president of each organization had sent a letter to each employee's home explaining the general nature of the research and asking for cooperation before the arrival of the research teams. At each organization, the research teams held meetings with various management and supervisory groups, the Scanlon Plan Screening Committee, and departmental groups of rank-and-file employees in order to explain the research in detail and to answer any questions. The research teams then handed the questionnaires to the employees as they left work at the end of each shift and collected those questionnaires which were returned the following day or night. The questionnaires were handed to the employees in envelopes addressed to the Department of Psychology, Michigan State University. Stamped envelopes addressed in this manner were provided for those employees who were absent when the questionnaire was administered.

The employees were not asked to sign their names, but enough detailed

185

"background" questions were on the questionnaire that identification would clearly have been no major problem. The research teams mentioned this fact in their meetings with the employees, but guaranteed their confidentiality, emphasizing that the individual questionnaires would be kept at Michigan State University. It was specifically emphasized that no one employed by any of the organizations involved in the research would see or be informed about any individual questionnaire response.

Sample. The type of industry, number of plants, and number of respondents for each of the organizations participating in the survey are presented in Appendix Table 1.

As indicated, a total of 3,884 questionnaires were distributed, and 2,636 (65 percent) usable questionnaires were returned. The median level of education for this sample was twelfth grade. Thirty-seven percent of the sample did not graduate from high school, and nineteen percent had some formal education beyond high school. Forty-six percent of the respondents were raised on farms; forty-six percent were raised in communities ranging in size from less than 2,000 to 100,000 in population; and eight percent were raised in cities with populations greater than 100,000. The mean age for this sample was thirty-five years, and the mean tenure was 3.89 years. Fifty-one percent of the subjects were males, and forty-nine percent were females.

APPENDIX TABLE 1

Organization	Type of Industry	Number of Plants	Number of Respondents
A	Manufacturers of beauty and dental shop equipment	4	176
B	Automotive supplier	3	241
C	Manufacturers of store fixtures, display items	1	96
D	Manufacture and sales of modern furniture systems	2	283
E	Manufacture of marine equipment	1	152
F	Shoe manufacturers	16	1688
	Total	27	2636

The Scanlon Plan, PDM, and Job Attitudes. Three broad variables were of primary interest in this study: (1) PDM through the Scanlon Plan, (2) PDM in the immediate job situation, and (3) job attitudes. The original questionnaire included 275 items, covering a broad range of job-related attitudes, perceptions of organizational characteristics, and demographic variables. Of relevance in this study were 44 of these items which were originally grouped into the following scales: participation through the Scanlon Plan (18 items), participation in the immediate job situation (5 items), job involvement[1] (11 items), motivation (6 items), identification with the organization[2] (4 items), and job satisfaction (2 items). These scales were revised on the basis of a series of item and cluster analyses. The scale revisions were based on decision rules which emphasized item content, item commonalities, item-total correlations, and α estimates of internal consistency. The revised scales included the following items:

Job Involvement ($\alpha = .87$)

1. My job means a lot more to me than just money.
2. I will stay overtime to finish a job, even if I am not a paid for it.
3. I am really interested in my work.
4. I would probably keep working even if I did not need the money.
5. The major satisfactions in my life come from my job.
6. The most important things that happen to me involve my work.
7. For me, the first few hours at work really fly by.
8. How much do you actually enjoy performing the daily activities that make up your job?
9. How much do you look forward to coming to work each day?

Motivation ($\alpha = .71$)

1. I feel bad when I make mistakes in my work.
2. How often do you really want to work hard at your job?
3. How much do you really want to do a good job?
4. I am really a perfectionist about my work.
5. How much do you feel your own personal satisfactions are related to how well you do your job?

Identification with the Organization ($\alpha = .68$)

1. How much is the welfare of your company related to your own personal welfare?
2. How much does the company's achievement of its goals help your achievement of your own personal goals?

187

Participation in the immediate job situation ($\alpha = .80$)

1. In general, how much say or influence do you have on how you perform your job?
2. To what extent are you able to decide how to do your job?
3. In general, how much say or influence do you have on what goes on in your work group?
4. In general, how much say or influence do you have on decisions which affect your job?
5. My superiors are receptive and listen to my ideas and suggestions.

Participation through the Scanlon Plan ($\alpha = .82$)

1. How much does the Scanlon Plan provide you with the opportunity to influence decisions which affect your job?
2. How often are the people in your work group given the real reasons why their suggestions were not acted on?
3. How much is it worth your effort to think up and offer suggestions to the production and screening committees?
4. How effective are the production and screening committees in improving company efficiency?
5. It's not really worth it to offer suggestions to the production and screening committees.

The occupational status classification was based on subject reports of job titles and organization charts. Employees with no subordinates were classified as rank-and-file; individuals occupying positions at and above first level of supervision were classified as management.

Education, Ego Need Gratification, and Job Attitudes. Two variables were used to index the extent of ENG provided by the job: (1) hierarchical level (HL), and (2) perceived ego need gratification (PENG). The HL measure was based on employee-reported job titles and organization charts. The PENG measure was based on responses to eight, five-point, Likert-type questionnaire items which asked the subjects to report the extent to which their jobs provided them with challenge, recognition, responsibility, freedom to make decisions, chances for promotion, opportunities to learn new skills, a sense of accomplishment, and feelings of importance. The mean of each subject's responses to these eight items was computed.

The measurement of IENG was based on responses to eight, five-point, Likert-type questionnaire items which asked the subjects to indicate the importance to them of the same job characteristics which were used to measure the PENG. That is, the subjects were asked to indicate on five-point scales how important it was to them that their jobs provide them with challenge, recognition, responsibility, freedom to make decisions, chances for promotion, opportunities to learn new skills, a sense of accomplishment, and feelings of importance. The mean of each subject's responses to these eight items was computed. For the analyses in which IENG served as a moderator variable, these means were trichotomized into approximately equal thirds of the distribution.

The job attitudes investigated were the same as those involved in the Ruh, Johnson, and Scontrino study: job involvement, motivation, and identification with the organization.[1]

The measure of education was based on a single questionnaire item which asked the subjects to indicate the number of years of school they completed.

Job Involvement, PDM, and Personal Background. The measures of JI, PDM, education, and community size were based on data collected from the SPA/MSU "You and Your Job Survey."

The job behavior measures were based on data collected from the largest of the six companies in which questionnaire data were collected. Performance data were collected for a sample of 238 blue-collar employees from two of this company's plants. Absenteeism data were collected for 398 employees from the same two plants, and turnover data were collected for all 1,662 of this company's employees from whom questionnaire data had been collected.

Questionnaire scales were constructed to measure JI, PDM, and community size through a series of item and cluster analyses. All these items were five-point, Likert-type questions. The items were initially grouped into clusters on the basis of face validity and the results of earlier analyses. Items were then eliminated and regrouped on the basis of inter-item correlations, item-cluster correlations, and alpha estimates of internal consistency.

The JI scale initially consisted of ten items, seven of which were from Lodahl and Kejner's original scale. Eight items were retained in the final scale. The median inter-item and item-cluster correlations for this final scale were .36 and .64, respectively. The alpha estimate of reliability was .81. All five of the items in the original PDM scale were retained. These items were the same as those used in "The Scanlon Plan, PDM, and Job Attitudes." The median inter-item and item-cluster correlations for this scale were .48 and .69, respectively. The alpha estimate was .80. All three of the original items in the community size scale were also retained. These items asked the subject to indicate the size of community in which he spent his early life,

189

the size of community in which he was currently living, and the size of community in which he preferred to live on five-point scales ranging from (1) farm to (5) cities larger than 100,000 in populations. The median inter-item and item-cluster correlations for this scale were .45 and .75, respectively, and the alpha estimate of reliability was .75.

Education and community size were trichotomized for those analyses for which they served as moderator variables. Education was trichotomized into the following categories: high—some college and beyond, approximately nineteen percent of the sample; medium—high school graduates, approximately forty-five percent of the sample; low = less than high school graduate—thirty-six percent of the sample. The community size measure was trichotomized into approximately the top, middle, and bottom thirds of the distribution.

Job performance was measured by averaging weekly productivity, expressed as a percentage of engineered standards, over a twenty-week period beginning seventeen months subsequent to the collection of questionnaire data. The weekly productivity data were adjusted for leaves of absence, machine down time, and other work stoppages not under the control of the worker. Performance ranged from 36.5 percent to 162 percent of standard.

Absenteeism was measured by the proportion of hours absent to total hours worked for the same twenty-week period for which the performance data were collected. The absenteeism measure was also adjusted for vacations, layoffs, and plant shutdowns. This measure ranged from 0.0 to .147. The turnover measure reflected voluntary terminations during the twenty-two months immediately following the collection of questionnaire data.

PDM, Values, and Job Attitudes. Nine of the values investigated were measured with the Rokeach Value Survey.[2] Rokeach defines a value as an "enduring belief that a specific mode of conduct (instrumental value) or an end state of existence (terminal value) is personally and socially preferrable to alternate modes of conduct or end states of existence."[3] Each subject was asked to rank order eighteen instrumental and eighteen terminal values according to their importance to him. Six of the values used in this study —self-controlled, responsible, independent, ambitious, capable, and imaginative—were instrumental values; and three—freedom, equality, and a sense of accomplishment—were terminal values. A tenth value, importance of participation, was measured by the following five-point, Likert-type questionnaire items:

How important to you is:

1. Everyone in the company, no matter how low his status level, having a say in the decisions affecting his job?
2. Being able to decide how to do your job?

PDM, job involvement, motivation, and identification with the organization were measured as in the Ruh, Johnson, and Scontrino study.[4]

In order to investigate the moderating effects of values on the relationships between participation in decision making and job attitudes, the sample was trichotomized into "high," "medium," and "low" subgroups for each value. These subgroups corresponded as closely as possible to the top, middle, and bottom thirds of the distributions. The correlations between participation in decision making and job attitudes were then computed within each of the subgroups. The hypothesis predicts that the rank order of the correlations should decrease monotonically from the "high" to the "low" value subgroups.

In addition, because previous research[5] indicated that the moderating effects of employee values might be restricted to blue-collar workers, the data were analyzed separately for rank-and-file workers and managers.

APPENDIX NOTES

1. Ruh, Johnson, and Scontrino, 1972.
2. Rokeach, 1968.
3. Ibid., p. 160.
4. Ruh, Johnson, and Scontrino, 1972.
5. Blood and Hulin, 1967.

191

REFERENCES

Adorno, T. W., Frenkel-Brunswick, Levinson, D., and Sanfor, R. *The Authoritarian Personality*. New York: Harper, 1950.

Allport, F. *Theories of Perception and the Concept of Structure*. New York: John Wiley & Sons Inc., 1954.

Argyris, C. *Integrating the Individual and the Organization*. New York: John Wiley & Sons Inc., 1964.

Aronoff, J. *Psychological Needs and Cultural Systems*. New York: Van Nostrand, 1967.

Aronoff, J., and Messe, L. "Experiments on the Effects of Personality Processes on Small Group Structure," unpublished manuscript, Michigan State University, 1969.

Atkinson, J. *An Introduction to Motivation*. New York: Van Nostrand, 1964.

Backman, J., Bowers, D., and Marcus, P. "Bases of Supervisory Power: A Comparative Study in Five Organizational Settings." Paper delivered at A.P.A. Convention, 1965; also in *Control in Organizations*, edited by A.S. Tannenbaum. New York: McGraw-Hill Book Company, 1968.

Backman, J., Smith, C., and Slesinger, J. "Control, Performance, and Satisfaction: An Analysis of Structural and Individual Effects," *Journal of Personality and Social Psychology* (1966), 4: 127–36.

Blood, M., and Hulin, C. "Alienation, Environmental Characteristics, and Worker Responses," *Journal of Applied Psychology* (1967), 51: 284–90.

Bowers, D. "Organizational Control in an Insurance Company," *Sociometry* (1964), 27: 230–44.

Chamberlain, J. "Everyman a Capitalist, *Life* (Dec. 23, 1946), pp. 93–94.

Coch, L., and French, J. "Overcoming Resistance to Change," *Human Relations* (1948), 1: 512–32.

Davenport, R. "Enterprise for Everyman," *Fortune* (1950), pp. 50–58.

Day, R., and Hamblin, R. "Some Effects of Close and Punitive Styles of Supervision," *American Journal of Sociology* (1964), 69: 499–510.

Doud, E. M. "The Scanlon Plan," *Management Record* (June 1955), 17: 236–239.

Farris, G. F. "Organizational Factors and Individual Performance: A Longitudinal Study," *Journal of Applied Psychology* (1969), 53: 87–92.

Farris, G. F. "A Predictive Study of Turnover," *Personnel Psychology* (1971), 24: 311–28.

Farris, G. F., and Lim, F. G. "Effects of Performance on Leadership, Cohesiveness, Influence, Satisfaction, and Subsequent Performance," *Journal of Applied Psychology* (1969), 53: 490–97.

Fleishman, E. A. "Attitude Versus Skill Factors in Work Group Productivity," *Personnel Psychology* (1965), 18: 253–66.

French, J., Israel, J., and As, D. "An Experiment on Participation in a Norwegian Factory," *Human Relations* (1960), 13 (1): 3–19.

192

Gilson, T. Q., and Lefcowitz, M. J. "A Plant-wide Productivity Bonus in a Small Factory. Study of an Unsuccessful Case," *Industrial and Labor Relations Review* (1957), 10: 284–96.

Goodman, R. K., Wakeley, J. H., and Ruh, R. A. "What Employees Think of the Scanlon Plan," *Personnel* (1972), 49: 22–99.

Graves, C. W. "Deterioration of Work Standards," *Harvard Business Review* (1966), vol. 44.

Gray, R. B. "The Scanlon Plan—A Case Study," *British Journal of Industrial Relations* (1971), 9: 291–313

Guilford, J. P. *Psychometric Methods.* New York: McGraw-Hill Book Company, 1954.

Haythorn, W., Haefner, D., Couch, A., and Carter, L. "The Effects of Varying Combinations of Authoritarian Leaders and Followers," *Journal of Abnormal and Social Psychology* (1956), 53: 210–19.

Helfgott, R. "Group Wage Incentives: Experience with the Scanlon Plan." New York: Industrial Relations Counselors, Industrial Relations memo no. 141, 1962.

Herzberg, F. *Work and the Nature of Man.* Cleveland: The World Publishing Co., 1966

Hulin, C., and Blood, M. "Job Enlargement, Individual Differences and Worker Responses, *Psychology Bulletin* (1968), 69 (1): 41–55.

Indik, B., Georgopoulous, B., and Seashore, S. "Superior-Subordinate Relationships and Performance," *Personnel Psychology* (1961), 14: 357–74.

Jehring, J. "A Contrast Between Two Approaches to Total System Incentives," *California Management Review* (1967), 10: 7–14.

Katz, D., Maccoby, N., Gurin, G., and Floor, L. *Productivity, Supervision and Morale Among Railroad Workers.* Ann Arbor: Survey Research Center, University of Michigan, 1951.

Katz, D., Maccoby, N., and Morse, N. *Productivity, Supervision and Morale in an Office Situation.* Ann Arbor: Survey Research Center, University of Michigan, 1950.

Lawler, E. E. "Job Attitudes and Employee Motivation: Theory, Research, and Practice, *Personnel Psychology* (1970), 23 (2): 223–37.

Lawler, E., and Hackman, R. "Impact of Employee Participation in the Development of Pay Incentive Plans: A Field Experiment," *Journal of Applied Psychology* (1969), 53: 467–71.

Lawler, E., and Hall, D. "The Relationships of Job Characteristics to Job Involvement, Satisfaction and Intrinsic Motivation," *Journal of Applied Psychology* (1970), 54: 305–12.

Lawrence, P., and Lorsch, J. *Organization and Environment.* Homewood, Ill.: Richard D. Irwin, Inc., 1967.

Lawrence, L., and Smith, P. "Group Decision and Employee Participation," *Journal of Applied Psychology* (1955), 39: 334–37.

Lesieur, F. G. "Local Union Experiences with a Cooperation Plan," *Proceedings of the Fourth Annual Meeting of the Industrial Relations Research Association* (1952), pp. 174–81.

Lesieur, F. G., and Puckett, E. "The Scanlon Plan: Past, Present, and Future," *Proceedings of the Twenty-First Annual Meeting of the Industrial Relations Research Association* (1958), pp. 71–80.

Lesieur, F. G., and Puckett, E. "The Scanlon Plan Has Proved Itself," *Harvard Business Review* (1969), 47: 109–18.

Levine, J., and Butler, J. "Lecture vs. Group Decision in Changing Behavior," *Journal of Applied Psychology* (1952), 36: 29–33.

Lewin, K. "Group Decision and Social Change," *Readings in Social Psychology*, rev. ed., edited by G. E. Swanson, T. Newcomb, and E. Hartley. New York: Holt, 1947, pp. 459–73.

Lewin, K., Lippitt, R., and White, R. "Patterns of Aggressive Behavior in Experimentally Created Social Climates, *Journal of Social Psychology* (1939), 10: 271–99.

Likert, R. *New Patterns of Management*. New York: McGraw-Hill Book Company, 1961.

Likert, R. *The Human Organization*. New York: McGraw-Hill Book Company, 1967.

Litwin, G. H., and Stringer, R. A. *Motivation and Organizational Climate*. Boston: Harvard Business School, 1968.

Lodahl, T., and Kejner, M. "The Definition and Measurement of Job Involvement," *Journal of Applied Psychology* (1965), 49: 24–33.

Lowin, A. "Participative Decision Making: A Model, Literature Critique and Prescriptions for Research, *Organizational Behavior and Human Performance* (1968), 3: 68–106.

Lowin, A., and Craig, J. "The Influence of Performance on Managerial Style: An Experimental Object-Lesson in the Ambiguity of Correlational Data," *Organizational Behavior and Human Performance* (1968), 3: 440–58.

McCurdy, H. G., and Eber, H. W. "Democratic Versus Authoritarian: A Further Investigation of Group Problem-Solving, *Journal of Personality* (1953), 22: 258–69.

McGregor, D. *The Human Side of Enterprise*. New York: McGraw-Hill Book Company, 1960.

MacKinney, A. C., Wernimont, P. F., and Galitz, W. O. "Has Specialization Reduced Job Satisfaction?" *Personnel* (1962), 39(1): 8–17.

March, J., and Simon, H. *Organizations*. New York: John Wiley & Sons, Inc., 1958.

Marrow, A., Bowers, D., and Seashore, S. *Management by Participation*. New York: Harper & Row, 1967.

Maurer, J. G. "The Relationship of Work Role Involvement to Job Characteristics with Higher-Order Need Potential," doctoral dissertation, Michigan State University, 1967.

Miles, R. "Human Relations or Human Resources," *Harvard Business Review* (1965), 42: 148–63.

Missumi, J. "Experimental Studies on Group Dynamics in Japan," *Psychologia* (1959), 2: 229–35.

194

Morse, N., and Reimer, E. "The Experimental Change of a Major Organizational Variable," *Journal of Abnormal and Social Psychology* (1956), 52: 120–29.

Patchen, M. "Participation in Decision Making and Motivation: What Is the Relation?" *Personnel Administration* (1964), pp. 24–31.

Patchen, M. *Some Questionnaire Measures of Employee Motivation and Morale.* Ann Arbor: Monograph no. 41, Survey Research Center, The University of Michigan, 1965.

Patchen, M. "Labor Management Consultation at TVA: Its Impact on Employees," *Administrative Science Quarterly* (1965), 10: 149–74.

Patchen, M. *Participation, Achievement and Involvement on the Job.* Englewood Cliffs, N.J.: Prentice-Hall, Inc., 1970.

Puckett, E. "Productivity Achievements—A Measure of Success," in *The Scanlon Plan: A Frontier in Labor-Management Cooperation,* edited by F. Lesieur, pp. 109–17. Cambridge, Mass.: MIT Press, 1958.

Rokeach, M. *Beliefs, Attitudes, and Values: A Theory of Organization and Change.* San Francisco: Jossey-Bass, 1968.

Rokeach, M., and Parker, S. "Values as Social Indicators of Poverty and Race Relations in America," *The Annals of the American Academy of Political and Social Science* (1970), 388: 97–111.

Ruh, R. A., Johnson, R. H., and Scontrino, M. P. "The Scanlon Plan, Participation in Decision Making, and Job Attitudes," *Journal of Industrial and Organizational Psychology* (1973), 1: 36–45.

Ruh, R. A., Wakeley, J. H., and Morrison, J. C. "Education, Ego Need Gratification, and Attitudes Toward the Job," unpublished manuscript, Michigan State University, 1972.

Ruh, R. A., Wallace, R. L., and Frost, C. F. "Management Attitudes and the Scanlon Plan," *Industrial Relations* (1973), 12: 282–88.

Sales, S. M. "A Laboratory Investigation of the Effectiveness of Two Industrial Supervisory Dimensions," master's thesis, Cornell University, 1964.

Scanlon, J. M. "Profit Sharing under Collective Bargaining: Three Case Studies," *Industrial and Labor Relations Review* (1948), 2: 58–75.

Schein, E. H. *Organizational Psychology,* Englewood Cliffs, N.J.: Prentice-Hall, Inc., 1971.

Schultz, G. P., and Crisara, R. P. *Cases in Industrial Peace under Collective Bargaining: The LaPointe Machine Tool Company and the United Steelworkers of America,* Case Study No. 10, Washington, D. C., 1952.

Seashore, S., and Bowers, D. *Changing the Structure and Functioning of an Organization: Report of a Field Experiment.* Ann Arbor: Institute for Social Research, 1963.

Shaw, M. "A Comparison of Two Types of Leadership in Various Communication Nets," *Journal of Abnormal and Social Psychology* (1955), 50: 127–34.

Siegel, A. L., and Ruh, R. A. "Job Involvement, Participation in Decision Making, Personal Background, and Job Behavior," *Organizational Behavior and Human Performance* (1973), 9: 318–27.

Smith, C., and Ari, O. N. "Organizational Control Structure and Member Consensus," *American Journal of Sociology* (May 1964), 69 (6): 623–38.

Smith, C., and Jones, G. "The Role of the Interaction-Influence System in a Planned Organizational Change," in *Control in Organizations,* edited by A. S. Tannenbaum. New York: McGraw-Hill Book Company, 1968.

Smith, C., and Tannenbaum, A. "Organizational Control Structure: A Comparative Analysis," *Human Relations* (1963), 16: 299–316.

Spector, P., and Suttell, B. *An Experimental Comparison of the Effectiveness of Three Patterns of Leadership Behavior.* Washington, D.C. American Institute for Research, 1957.

Strauss, G. "Group Dynamics and Intergroup Relations," in W. F. Whyte, *Money and Motivation,* pp. 90–96. New York: Harper & Row, 1955.

Strauss, G. "Some Notes on Power-Equalization," in *The Social Science of Organizations,* edited by H. Leavitt. Englewood Cliffs, N.J.: Prentice-Hall, Inc., 1963.

Strauss, G. P., and Sayles, L. R. "The Scanlon Plan: Some Organizational Problems," *Human Organization* (1957), 16: 15–22.

Tait, R. C. "Some Experiences with a Union-Management Cooperation Plan," *Proceedings of the Fourth Annual Meeting of the Industrial Relations Research Association* (1952), pp. 167–73.

Tannenbaum, A. S. (ed.). *Control in Organizations.* New York: McGraw-Hill Book Company, 1968

Tannenbaum, A. S., and Allport, F. H. "Personality Structure and Group Structure; an Interpretative Study of Their Relationship Through an Event-Structure Hypothesis," *Journal of Abnormal and Social Psychology* (1956), 53: 272–80.

Tannenbaum, A. S., and Smith, C. "Effects of Member Influence in an Organization: Phenomenology Versus Organization Structure," *Journal of Abnormal and Social Psychology* (1964), 69: 401–10.

Tosi, H. "A Re-evaluation of Personality as a Determinant of the Effects of Participation," *Personnel Psychology* (1970), 23: 91–100.

Turner, A., and Lawrence, P. *Industrial Jobs and the Worker: An Investigation of Response to Task Attributes.* Boston: Harvard University Graduate School of Business Administration, 1965.

Vroom, V. H. "Ego-Involvement, Job Satisfaction, and Job Performance," *Personnel Psychology* (1962), 15: 159–77.

Vroom, V. "Some Personality Determinants of the Effects of Participation," *Journal of Abnormal and Social Psychology* (1959), 59: 322–27.

Wallace, R. L. "A Comparative Study of Attitude Scores of Managers Toward Employees and Toward Selected Leadership Policies in Groups of Firms Which Have Either Discontinued or Retained Cost Reduction Sharing Plans," doctoral dissertation, Michigan State University, 1971.

White, J. K., Ruh, R. A., and Morrison, J. C. "Participation in Decision Making, Values, and Attitudes Toward the Job," unpublished manuscript, Michigan State University, 1972.

Woodward, J. *Industrial Organization: Theory and Practice.* London: Oxford University Press, 1965.

Yuchtman, E. "Control in an Insurance Company: Cause or Effect," in *Control in Organizations,* edited by A. S. Tannenbaum, pp. 125–28. New York: McGraw-Hill Book Company, 1968.